JEWISH LEARNING INSTITUTE

ב"ה

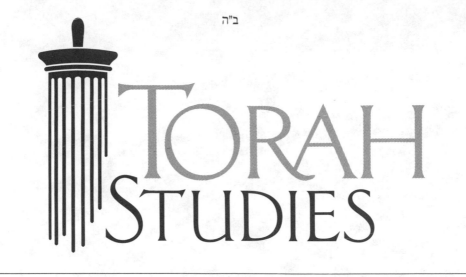

Torah Studies

Season One 5777

Student Manual

The ROHR JEWISH LEARNING INSTITUTE
gratefully acknowledges
the pioneering support of

George & Pamela
Rohr

Since its inception,
the JLI has been
a beneficiary of the vision,
generosity, care, and concern
of the Rohr family.

In the merit of
the tens of thousands of hours
of Torah study
by JLI students worldwide,
may they be blessed with health,
Yiddishe nachas from all their loved ones,
and extraordinary success
in all of their endeavors.

Rivky Deren Berman was born in 1987 in Springfield, Massachusetts to Chabad emissaries in Western and Southern New England, Rabbi Yisrael and Vivi Deren. From a young age, Rivky absorbed the warm Jewish atmosphere that permeated her home, and acquired her parents' dedication to sharing the beauty of Judaism with her community.

Rivky was born with Bloom syndrome, a condition that affected her growth and presented lifelong medical challenges. Despite her condition, Rivky always maintained an upbeat attitude, strong faith in G-d, and relentless persistence. A talented and caring organizer, she never, never let her illness prevent her from living an active life and sharing her optimism, friendship, and wisdom with others. With her remarkable ability to connect with others—especially those struggling with handicaps and special needs in their own lives—she inspired thousands with blog posts and personal communication in every venue available to her.

After a successful lung transplant, she married Rabbi Shmulie Berman in the summer of 2012. The young couple moved to North Carolina as Chabad emissaries, where they helped with undergraduate programming at Chabad of Duke University, and were instrumental in the founding of Chabad at North Carolina State University. After being diagnosed with lymphoma in 2015, Rivky continued to organize and serve her community from the confines of her hospital bed.

Even after her tragic passing at the young age of 29, Rivky's influence continues to inspire, as thousands watch and gain inspiration from her moving videos and personal story, finding faith in Hashem and strength to overcome life's challenges with cheer and valor.

Contents

1. **NOACH:** The Raven and the Dove 11
   Dealing with a Personal Flood

2. **LECH LECHA:** The Top Ten Percent 31
   Behind the Commandment to Tithe

3. **VAYERA:** Sorry, No Shortcuts Here 57
   Personal Investment in Judaism

4. **CHAYEI SARAH:** Matchmaker, Make Me a Match. . . 81
   Dating in the Orthodox Jewish Community

5. **TOLDOS:** Truth or Consequences 115
   Is It Ever Okay to Lie?

6. **VAYETZEI:** The Nighttime Plea 139
   Finding Hope in the Darkness

7. **VAYISHLACH:** The Principles of Punishment 157
   When Discipline Becomes Revenge

8. **VAYESHEV:** Do Something, Anything 181
   The Key to Getting Unstuck

9. **CHANUKAH:** The Psychology of the Chanukah Candles . 205
   Behaviorism vs. Cognitivism

10. **VAYIGASH:** My Brother's Keeper 225
    Mutual Responsibility in Judaism

11. **VAYECHI:** When Is Moshiach Coming? 245
    Growing Out of the Exile Mentality

NOACH

The Raven and the Dove

Dealing with a Personal Flood

*Dedicated in loving memory of Leah bat Shlomo Zev HaKohen
on the occasion of her yahrtzeit, 24 Tishrei, 5776*

PARASHA OVERVIEW
Noach

G-d instructs Noah—the only righteous man in a world consumed by violence and corruption—to build a large wooden teivah ("ark"), coated within and without with pitch. A great deluge, says G-d, will wipe out all life from the face of the earth; but the ark will float upon the water, sheltering Noah and his family, and two members (male and female) of each animal species.

Rain falls for 40 days and nights, and the waters churn for 150 days more before calming and beginning to recede. The ark settles on Mount Ararat, and from its window Noah dispatches a raven, and then a series of doves, "to see if the waters were abated from the face of the earth." When the ground dries completely—exactly one solar year (365 days) after the onset of the Flood—G-d commands Noah to exit the teivah and repopulate the earth.

Noah builds an altar and offers sacrifices to G-d. G-d swears never again to destroy all of mankind because of their deeds, and sets the rainbow as a testimony of His new covenant with man. G-d also commands Noah regarding the sacredness of life: murder is deemed a capital offense, and while man is permitted to eat the meat of animals, he is forbidden to eat flesh or blood taken from a living animal.

Noah plants a vineyard and becomes drunk on its produce. Two of Noah's sons, Shem and Japheth, are blessed for covering up their father's nakedness, while his third son, Ham, is punished for taking advantage of his debasement.

The descendants of Noah remain a single people, with a single language and culture, for ten generations. Then they defy their Creator by building a greattower to symbolize their own invincibility; G-d confuses their language so that "one does not comprehend the tongue of the other," causing them to abandon their project and disperse across the face of the earth, splitting into seventy nations.

The Parshah of Noach concludes with a chronology of the ten generations from Noah to Abram (later Abraham), and the latter's journey from his birthplace of Ur Casdim to Charan, on the way to the land of Canaan

Tale of Two Birds

Aftermath

TEXT 1

Bereishit (Genesis) 8:6–14

וַיְהִי מִקֵּץ אַרְבָּעִים יוֹם וַיִּפְתַּח נֹחַ אֶת חַלּוֹן הַתֵּבָה אֲשֶׁר עָשָׂה:

וַיְשַׁלַּח אֶת הָעֹרֵב וַיֵּצֵא יָצוֹא וָשׁוֹב עַד יְבֹשֶׁת הַמַּיִם מֵעַל הָאָרֶץ:

וַיְשַׁלַּח אֶת הַיּוֹנָה מֵאִתּוֹ לִרְאוֹת הֲקַלּוּ הַמַּיִם מֵעַל פְּנֵי הָאֲדָמָה:

וְלֹא מָצְאָה הַיּוֹנָה מָנוֹחַ לְכַף רַגְלָהּ וַתָּשָׁב אֵלָיו אֶל הַתֵּבָה כִּי מַיִם עַל פְּנֵי כָל הָאָרֶץ וַיִּשְׁלַח יָדוֹ וַיִּקָּחֶהָ וַיָּבֵא אֹתָהּ אֵלָיו אֶל הַתֵּבָה:

וַיָּחֶל עוֹד שִׁבְעַת יָמִים אֲחֵרִים וַיֹּסֶף שַׁלַּח אֶת הַיּוֹנָה מִן הַתֵּבָה:

וַתָּבֹא אֵלָיו הַיּוֹנָה לְעֵת עֶרֶב וְהִנֵּה עֲלֵה זַיִת טָרָף בְּפִיהָ וַיֵּדַע נֹחַ כִּי קַלּוּ הַמַּיִם מֵעַל הָאָרֶץ:

וַיִּיָּחֶל עוֹד שִׁבְעַת יָמִים אֲחֵרִים וַיְשַׁלַּח אֶת הַיּוֹנָה וְלֹא יָסְפָה שׁוּב אֵלָיו עוֹד:

וַיְהִי בְּאַחַת וְשֵׁשׁ מֵאוֹת שָׁנָה בָּרִאשׁוֹן בְּאֶחָד לַחֹדֶשׁ חָרְבוּ הַמַּיִם מֵעַל הָאָרֶץ וַיָּסַר נֹחַ אֶת מִכְסֵה הַתֵּבָה וַיַּרְא וְהִנֵּה חָרְבוּ פְּנֵי הָאֲדָמָה:

וּבַחֹדֶשׁ הַשֵּׁנִי בְּשִׁבְעָה וְעֶשְׂרִים יוֹם לַחֹדֶשׁ יָבְשָׁה הָאָרֶץ:

And it came to pass at the end of forty days, that Noah opened the window of the ark that he had made.

And he sent forth the raven, and it went out, back and forth until the waters dried up off the earth.

And he sent forth the dove from with him, to see whether the waters had abated from upon the surface of the earth.

But the dove found no resting place for the sole of its foot; so it returned to him to the ark because there was water upon the entire surface of the earth; so he stretched forth his hand and took it, and he brought it to him to the ark.

And he waited again another seven days, and he again sent forth the dove from the ark.

And the dove returned to him at eventide, and behold it had plucked an olive leaf in its mouth; so Noah knew that the water had abated from upon the earth.

And he again waited another seven days, and he sent forth the dove, and it no longer continued to return to him.

And it came to pass in the six hundredth and first year, in the first [month], on the first of the month, that the waters dried up from upon the earth, and Noah removed the covering of the ark, and he saw, and behold, the surface of the ground had dried up.

And in the second month, on the twenty-seventh day of the month, the earth was dry

Why a Raven and a Dove?

TEXT 2

Rabbi Naftali Zvi Yehuda Berlin, Netziv
1816-1893
Rabbi, dean of the Volozhin Yeshiva and author of several works of rabbinic literature in Lithuania. Born in Mir, into a family of Jewish scholars renowned for its Talmudic scholarship, Rabbi Berlin married into the famed Volozhin family, which led his path to the leadership of the Volzhin Yeshivah. A master teacher, Rabbi Berlin mentored a number of prominent rabbinic figures who led Eastern European Jewry until World War II. While he intended to travel to the Land of Israel, his medical condition made this impossible, and he passed in Warsaw in 1893.

Rabbi Naftali Zvi Yehuda Berlin, Ha'amek Davar, Bereishit 8:7

יש להתבונן למה שלח נח עופות אלה דווקא עורב ויונה. והלא יש עופות שפורחים טוב יותר מהם? ותו, מאין היה רשות לנח להוציאם מן התבה לפני זמן היציאה לכולם?

Think about it: Why did Noah choose specifically these birds, the raven and the dove? Are there no birds that fly better than them?

Furthermore, how did Noah have permission to let these two birds out of the ark before the time came for everyone else to leave?

A Bird Without a Mission

TEXT 3

Rabbi Chayim ibn Atar
(Or Hachayim)
1696–1743
Biblical exegete, kabbalist, and Talmudist. Rabbi Atar, born in Meknes, Morocco, was a prominent member of the Moroccan rabbinate and later immigrated to the Land of Israel. He is most famous for his *Or Hachayim*, a popular commentary on the Torah. The famed Jewish historian and bibliophile Rabbi Chaim Yosef David Azulai was among his most notable disciples.

Rabbi Chayim ibn Atar, Or Hachayim, *Bereishit 8:7*

"וישלח את העורב וגו'." צריך לדעת למה שלחו, ואם לראות הקלו המים היה לו לומר הכתוב הקלו המים כמו שאמר בשליחות היונה.

**A**nd he sent the raven, etc." Why did he send it? If the purpose was to see if the waters had abated, the verse should have stated so, as it did with the dove's mission.

Post-Flood Postal Service

TEXT 4

Rabbi Naftali Zvi Yehuda Berlin, Ibid.

על כן היה נראה לפי הפשט דעורב ויונה הללו לא היו מן הזוגות שנכנסו
להחיות זרע בדבר ה', אלא בשביל שהיה נח לפני מי המבול כאחד מן
השרים שמנהגם הי' גם אז לגדל עורבים ויונים...ונכנסו גם המה בכלל
וכל ביתך...

מנהג העורב הגדל בבית שלא לשלחו במרקחים. מה שאין כן יונה היא
מלומדת לכך לשאת מכתבים למרחוק ולהביא איזה דבר בפיו.על כן
כששלוח נח את העורב ובראותו מים סביב התבה לא הלך למרחוק
אלא יצא ושוב כמה פעמים סמוך לתבה אבל היונה המלומדת להביא
דבר שליחות גם מרחוק משום הכי כתיב בה "וישלח את היונה וגו'" כי
תעוף גם למרחוק.

I would suggest that this raven and dove were not among the pairs brought into the ark upon G-d's command for the purpose of breeding offspring. Rather, before the flood, Noah was a nobleman, and the custom then was for noblemen to raise ravens and doves... These birds entered the ark as part of Noah's household...

Home-grown ravens are not sent far, but doves are used to traveling long distances to carry letters and bring back various objects in its mouth. Thus, when Noah sent the raven and it saw only water, it stayed put rather than travel far. So he sent the dove, who was used to flying on faraway missions.

Bird Character

The Mean Raven

TEXT 5A

Tehillim (Psalms) 147:9

נוֹתֵן לִבְהֵמָה לַחְמָהּ לִבְנֵי עֹרֵב אֲשֶׁר יִקְרָאוּ:

He gives the animal its food, to the young ravens that call out.

TEXT 5B

Midrash Yalkut Shimoni, 846

ומנין לעורב שהוא אכזרי על בניו, שנאמר "מי יכין לעורב צידו כי ילדיו אל א-ל ישועו וגו'", ואומר "לבני עורב אשר יקראו", כשהעורב מוליד ילדיו לבנים, ואומר הזכר לנקבה שמא אחר בא עליה, ומואסין אותן ומניחין אותן, מה הקדוש ברוך הוא עושה? —מוציא מצואה שלהן יתושין ופורחין עליהן ואוכלין ומשחירין.

Yalkut Shimoni

A Midrash that covers the entire Biblical text. Its material is collected from all over rabbinic literature, including the Babylonian and Jerusalem Talmuds and various ancient Midrashic texts. It contains several passages from Midrashim that have been lost, as well as different versions of existing Midrashim. It is unclear when and by whom this Midrash was redacted.

How do we know that a raven is cruel to its children? The verse states, "Who prepares for the raven his prey, when his young cry out to G-d, etc." Furthermore, the verse states, "to the young ravens that call out." When a raven mothers children, the male says to the mother that perhaps some other *bird is the father, and rejects the children and abandons them. So what does G-d do? He brings forth mosquitos from their waste for them to eat and develop.*

TEXT 6

Talmud Tractate Sanhedrin 108

תנו רבנן: שלשה שמשו בתיבה וכולם לקו כלב ועורב וחם.

he Rabbis have taught: *There were three who cohabited in the ark, and each of them was stricken: The dog, the raven, and Cham.*

Babylonian Talmud
A literary work of monumental proportions that draws upon the legal, spiritual, intellectual, ethical, and historical traditions of Judaism. The 37 tractates of the Babylonian Talmud contain the teachings of the Jewish sages from the period after the destruction of the 2nd Temple through the 5th century CE. It has served as the primary vehicle for the transmission of the Oral Law and the education of Jews over the centuries; it is the entry point for all subsequent legal, ethical, and theological Jewish scholarship.

STORY

The Arizal once went with his colleagues to pray at the tomb of Rabbi Yehuda Bar Ilai. As they neared the tomb, a raven flew near and perched on a branch in front of the Arizal, and called out several times. The Arizal said, "This raven is a reincarnation of a certain wicked tax collector who was very cruel to the poor. His soul is being punished for his cruel behavior toward the poor, for snatching their clothing and property, and now he is begging me to pray for him."

Dove of Love

TEXT 7A

Shir Hashirim (Song of Songs) 1:15

הִנָּךְ יָפָה רַעְיָתִי הִנָּךְ יָפָה עֵינַיִךְ יוֹנִים:

ehold, you are comely, my beloved; behold, you are comely; your eyes are like doves.

TEXT 7B

Shir Hashirim Rabah, ad loc.

מה יונה זו תמה, כך ישראל נאים בהילוכן כשהן עולין לפעמי רגלים. מה יונה זו מצויינת כך ישראל מצויינין... מה יונה זו צנועה. כך ישראל צנועים... מה יונה זו משעה שמכרת בן זוגה עוד אינה ממירה אותו באחר, כך ישראל משעה שהכירו להקדוש ברוך הוא לא המירוהו באחר... מה יונה זו אף על פי שאת נוטל גוזליה מתחתיה אין מנחת שובכה לעולם. כך ישראל אף על פי שחרב בית המקדש לא בטלו שלוש רגלים בשנה. מה יונה זו מחדשת לה בכל חדש וחדש גרן. כך ישראל מחדשים להם בכל חדש תורה ומצוות ומעשים טובים. מה יונה זו משוגרת רוגליות הרבה וחוזרת לשובכה. כך ישראל... מה יונה זו הביאה אורה לעולם. כך ישראל מביאין אורה לעולם, שנאמר "והלכו גויים לאורך". ואימתי הביאה יונה אורה לעולם? בימי נח הדא הוא דכתיב "ותבא אליו היונה לעת ערב והנה עלה זית טרף בפיה וגו'".

*J*ust as a dove is wholesome, Israel is pleasant in their way when they travel to Jerusalem for the three holidays.

Just as a dove excels, Israel excels… Just as a dove is modest, Israel is modest… Just as a dove is faithful to its spouse, Israel is faithful to G-d. Just as a dove doesn't abandon its next, even if its chicks are taken from it, so too the Jewish people, though their Temple is destroyed, they don't abandon the three festivals.

Just as a dove hatches new offspring each month, the Jewish people renew each month Torah, mitzvot, and good deeds. Just as a dove travels great distances and returns to its nest, so too the Jewish people. Just as a dove brought light to the world, the Jewish people bring light to the world, as it is written, "And nations shall go by your light." Now, when did a dove bring light to the world? In the days of Noah, as it is written, "And the dove returned to him at eventide, and behold it had plucked an olive leaf in its mouth."

Shir Hashirim Rabah
A midrashic text and exegetical commentary on the book of Song of Songs. This Midrash explicates this biblical book based on the principle that its verses convey an allegory of the relationship between God and the people of Israel. It was compiled and edited in the Land of Israel during the 6th century.

TEXT 8

Leviticus 1:14

וְאִם מִן הָעוֹף עֹלָה קָרְבָּנוֹ לַה' וְהִקְרִיב מִן הַתֹּרִים אוֹ מִן בְּנֵי הַיּוֹנָה אֶת קָרְבָּנוֹ:

And if his sacrifice to G-d is a burnt offering from birds, he shall bring [it] from turtle doves or from young doves.

Eradicating Evil

TEXT 9A

Rabbi Chaim Tirer of Chernovitz, Be'er Mayim Chayim, Parashat Noach, §7

אמרו חכמינו ז"ל יצא ישוב שהיה הולך ומקיף סביבות התבה ולא הלך בשליחתו לפי שהיה חושדו וכו'. ולהבין מפני מה בחר נח מכל המינים שלא לשלוח אלא העורב? הלא ידע כי רשע הוא מאשר שימש בתבה, ואיך על ידו יאמר לו בשורה טובה? והלא איש טוב מבשר טוב כתיב ולא איש רע?

Our Sages of blessed memory have said that the raven encircled the ark and did not go to fulfill its errand because it suspected Noah concerning its mate, etc. Why, from all species, did Noah choose to send the raven? Didn't he know that the raven was wicked from the fact that it cohabited in the ark? How could Noah expect to hear good news *from such a creature? Doesn't the verse state, "A good person heralds good tidings," and not a wicked person?*

TEXT 9B

Rabbi Chaim Tirer of Chernovitz, Ibid.

ונראה בזה שזה ששלח את העורב לא היה כלל בתורת שליחות לומר לו אם חרבו פני אדמה והראיה שלהלן כתיב וישלח את היונה לראות הקלו המים מעל פני האדמה. וכאן לא כתוב זה כלל כי אם סתם וישלח את העורב ויצא יצוא ושוב.

והענין הוא כי הערב היא אותיות עברה. וגם עורב לבד מלא הוא אותיות בו רע וחסר בלא ו' הוא אותיות ברע. כי נשרש בו מדת הרע ועל כן שימש בתיבה שנאסר לו. וגם חז"ל אמרו העורב הזה הוא אכזרי על בניו וזה הכל שורש הרע.

ובפרט נח הצדיק שזן ופרנס י"ב חודש כל החיות והבהמות בצער גדול והיה גונח וכוהה דם מטרחתן כפרש"י ומאמר חכמינו ז"ל ודאי שלא היה יכול לסבול בריאה אכזרי כזאת. וכיון שזכה נח לפתוח פתח החלון בבחינת עין יפה... לא היה רוצה לדור עם נחש בכפיפה להחזיק אצלו שורש הרע ועל כן "וישלח את העורב" שלוחין ממש עשה לו לגרשו כדי שלא להיותו עמו בצוותא.

I would suggest that Noach did not send the raven on a mission to tell him if the earth had dried up. Proof of this is the fact that while, regarding the dove, the verse states, "He sent the dove to see if the waters had abated from upon the surface of the earth," here the verse writes nothing of the sort, just that "he sent forth the raven, and it went out, back and forth."

Rather, the intention was this: The word עורב [raven] is comprised of the same letters as the word עברה [anger]. Furthermore, עורב spelled out fully has the same letters as בו רע [wickedness within him]. Written in short form, ברע has the same letters as ברע [with evil]. For the trait of wickedness is ingrained in the raven. Therefore, it cohabited in the ark, though cohabitation was forbidden. Our Sages of blessed memory have said, "This raven is cruel to its children." All of this indicates the root of evil.

Noah was particularly righteous, for he sustained and fed all the animals in the ark for twelve months at great personal cost, to the point that he was "groaning and spitting blood" from their burden. He could not tolerate such a cruel creature ... and did not want to live in close quarters with the root of evil. So, he sent off the raven, banishing it so he would no longer have to be together with it.

Evil Before Good

TEXT 10

Rabbi Tzadok Hakohen of Lublin, Kometz Haminchah, Part Two, §24

ולכך הקדים נח שליחות העורב לעולם מן היונה כמו שקדם עשו ליעקב כי לעולם הקליפה קדמה לפרי .

herefore, Noah sent the raven and then the dove, just as Esau preceded Jacob, for the peel always grows before the fruit.

Rabbi Tzadok Hakohen Rabinowitz of Lublin
1823–1900
Chasidic master and thinker. Rabbi Tzadok was born into a Lithuanian rabbinic family and later joined the Chasidic movement. He was a follower of the Chasidic leaders Rabbi Mordechai Yosef Leiner of Izbica and Rabbi Leibel Eiger. He succeeded Rabbi Eiger after his passing and became a rebbe in Lublin, Poland. He authored many works on Jewish law, Chasidism, Kabbalah, and ethics, as well as scholarly essays on astronomy, geometry, and algebra.

Jewish Flood Insurance

Kindness and Strictness

TEXT 11

Rabbi Shneur Zalman of Liadi
(Alter Rebbe)
1745–1812

Chasidic rebbe, halachic authority, and founder of the Chabad movement. The Alter Rebbe was born in Liozna, Belarus, and was among the principal students of the Magid of Mezeritch. His numerous works include the *Tanya*, an early classic containing the fundamentals of Chabad Chasidism, and *Shulchan Aruch HaRav*, an expanded and reworked code of Jewish law.

Rabbi Shneur Zalman of Liadi, Tanya, Igeret Hakodesh, Epistle 15

והנה כללות הי' ספירות שבנשמת האדם נודע לכל [בדרך כלל] שהמדות נחלקות בדרך כלל לז' מדות וכל פרטי המדות שבאדם באות מאחת מז' מדות אלו שהן שורש כל המדות וכללותן שהן מדת החסד להשפיע בלי גבול ומדת הגבורה לצמצם מלהשפיע כל לך או שלא להשפיע כלל.

Now, as regards the totality of the ten sefirot as they are in the soul of man, it is known to all that the attributes are generally divided into seven (emotive) attributes (midot), and all the specific traits in man derive from one of these seven attributes. These attributes are the root of all the traits. They are the attribute of chesed—to share without limit, and the attribute of gevurah—to withhold from sharing so much, or from sharing altogether.

TEXT 12

Tanya, Igeret Hakodesh, op. cit.,

בכלל עובדי ה' יש ב' בחינות ומדרגות חלוקות, מצד שורש נשמתם למעלה (במידות האלוקיות) מבחינת ימין (חסד) ושמאל (דין): דהיינו, שבחינת שמאל היא מידת הצמצום... ממידה זו נמשכה (הגיעה) גם כן בחינת הצמצום והגבול בעבודת ה', כמו בצדקה... המבזבז אל יבזבז יותר מחומש, ושארי מצוות די לו שיוצא ידי חובתו...אך בחינת ימין היא מידת החסד וההתפשטות בעבודת ה', בהתרחבות בלי צמצום והסתר כלל... וגם בלי צמצום וגבול כלל, ואין מעצור לרוח נדבתו בין בצדקה, ובין בתלמוד תורה ושארי מצוות, ולא די לו לצאת ידי חובתו בלבד, אלא עד בלי די.

Among Divine servants, there are two degrees and levels that, depending on the root of their souls above, are distinct in relation to the categories of the right and the left.

That is, the characteristic of the left is the trait of contraction (tzimtzum) and concealment ... From this attribute derives also the aspect of contraction (tzimtzum) and limitation in Divine service; for example, with charity ... that "one should not expend more than one fifth"; and, likewise, as regards the study of Torah and the other commandments—he makes do with discharging his duty, the definite duty to which the Torah obliges him...

By contrast, the characteristic of the right is the attribute of grace (chesed) and extension in Divine service by way of expansion, without any contraction and concealment whatsoever… There is no restraint to the spirit of his generosity—whether it be with respect to charity, the study of Torah, or other commandments. He does not suffice in discharging his obligation only, but to the extent of "never sufficient…"

Rebuilding after the Flood

TEXT 13

Rabbi Shneur Zalman of Liadi, Tanya, Sha'ar Hayichud, ch. 4

והנה בסידור שבחיו של הקדוש ברוך הוא כתיב "הגדול הגבור כו'" ופירוש הגדול היא מדת חסד והתפשטות החיות בכל העולמות וברואים לאין קץ ותכלית להיות ברואים מאין ליש וקיימים בחסד חנם ונקראת גדולה כי באה מגדולתו של הקדוש ברוך הוא בכבודו ובעצמו כי גדול ה' ולגדולתו אין חקר ולכן משפיע גם כן חיות והתהוות מאין ליש לעולמות וברואים אין קץ שטבע הטוב להטיב.

When listing the praises of the Holy One, blessed be He, it is written, "Hagadol" (the Great), "Hagibor" (the Mighty), etc. "Hagadol" refers to the attribute of chesed (kindness) and spreading unending, unlimited life-force into all worlds and created things. This life creates all being from nothing into something and allows them to exist through gratuitous kindness. The attribute of chesed is called gedulah (greatness) for it comes from the greatness of the Holy One, blessed be He, in His Glory,

for "G-d is great and His greatness is unsearchable."
Because G-d is so great, He also injects life and cre-
ates an unlimited number of worlds and creatures
from nothing to something, for "it is the nature of the
Beneficent to do good."

2

LECH LECHA

The Top Ten Percent

Behind the Commandment to Tithe

Dedicated loving memory of Mrs. Charlotte Rohr

לע"נ האשה החשובה מרת שרה ע"ה בת ר' יקותיאל יהודה ומרת לאה הי"ד | נפטרה י' מרחשון תשס"ח

PARASHA OVERVIEW
Lech Lecha

G-d speaks to Abram, commanding him, "Go from your land, from your birthplace and from your father's house, to the land which I will show you." There, G-d says, he will be made into a great nation. Abram and his wife, Sarai, accompanied by his nephew Lot, journey to the land of Canaan, where Abram builds an altar and continues to spread the message of a one G-d.

A famine forces the first Jew to depart for Egypt, where beautiful Sarai is taken to Pharaoh's palace; Abram escapes death because they present themselves as brother and sister. A plague prevents the Egyptian king from touching her, and convinces him to return her to Abram and to compensate the brother-revealed-as-husband with gold, silver and cattle.

Back in the land of Canaan, Lot separates from Abram and settles in the evil city of Sodom, where he falls captive when the mighty armies of Chedorlaomer and his three allies conquer the five cities of the Sodom Valley. Abram sets out with a small band to rescue his nephew, defeats the four kings, and is blessed by Malki-Zedek the king of Salem (Jerusalem).

G-d seals the Covenant Between the Parts with Abram, in which the exile and persecution (galut) of the people of Israel is foretold, and the Holy Land is bequeathed to them as their eternal heritage.

Still childless ten years after their arrival in the Land, Sarai tells Abram to marry her maidservant Hagar. Hagar conceives, becomes insolent toward her mistress, and then flees when Sarai treats her harshly; an angel convinces her to return, and tells her that her son will father a populous nation. Ishmael is born in Abram's eighty-sixth year.

Thirteen years later, G-d changes Abram's name to Abraham ("father of multitudes"), and Sarai's to Sarah ("princess"), and promises that a son will be born to them; from this child, whom they should call Isaac ("will laugh"), will stem the great nation with which G-d will establish His special bond. Abraham is commanded to circumcise himself and his descendants as a "sign of the covenant between Me and you." Abraham immediately complies, circumcising himself and all the males of his household.

Abraham's Tithes

The War

TEXT 1A

Bereishit (Genesis) 14:1–2

וַיְהִי בִּימֵי אַמְרָפֶל מֶלֶךְ שִׁנְעָר אַרְיוֹךְ מֶלֶךְ אֶלָּסָר כְּדָרְלָעֹמֶר מֶלֶךְ עֵילָם
וְתִדְעָל מֶלֶךְ גּוֹיִם:

עָשׂוּ מִלְחָמָה אֶת בֶּרַע מֶלֶךְ סְדֹם וְאֶת בִּרְשַׁע מֶלֶךְ עֲמֹרָה שִׁנְאָב מֶלֶךְ
אַדְמָה וְשֶׁמְאֵבֶר מֶלֶךְ צְבוֹיִים וּמֶלֶךְ בֶּלַע הִיא צֹעַר:

Now it came to pass in the days of Amraphel the king of Shinar, Arioch the king of Ellasar, Chedorlaomer the king of Elam, and Tidal the king of Goyim.

That they waged war with Bera the king of Sodom and with Birsha the king of Gomorrah, Shineab the king of Admah, and Shemeber the king of Zeboiim, and the king of Bela, which is Zoar.

Abraham the Hero

TEXT 1B

Ibid., 8–12

וַיֵּצֵא מֶלֶךְ סְדֹם וּמֶלֶךְ עֲמֹרָה וּמֶלֶךְ אַדְמָה וּמֶלֶךְ צְבוֹיִם וּמֶלֶךְ בֶּלַע הוּא צֹעַר וַיַּעַרְכוּ אִתָּם מִלְחָמָה בְּעֵמֶק הַשִּׂדִּים:

אֵת כְּדָרְלָעֹמֶר מֶלֶךְ עֵילָם וְתִדְעָל מֶלֶךְ גּוֹיִם וְאַמְרָפֶל מֶלֶךְ שִׁנְעָר וְאַרְיוֹךְ מֶלֶךְ אֶלָּסָר אַרְבָּעָה מְלָכִים אֶת הַחֲמִשָּׁה:

וְעֵמֶק הַשִּׂדִּים בֶּאֱרֹת בֶּאֱרֹת חֵמָר וַיָּנֻסוּ מֶלֶךְ סְדֹם וַעֲמֹרָה וַיִּפְּלוּ שָׁמָּה וְהַנִּשְׁאָרִים הֶרָה נָּסוּ:

וַיִּקְחוּ אֶת כָּל רְכֻשׁ סְדֹם וַעֲמֹרָה וְאֶת כָּל אָכְלָם וַיֵּלֵכוּ:

וַיִּקְחוּ אֶת לוֹט וְאֶת רְכֻשׁוֹ בֶּן אֲחִי אַבְרָם וַיֵּלֵכוּ וְהוּא יֹשֵׁב בִּסְדֹם:

And the king of Sodom and the king of Gomorrah and the king of Admah and the king of Zeboïm, and the king of Bela, which is Zoar, came forth, and they engaged them in battle in the valley of Siddim.

With Chedorlaomer the king of Elam, and Tidal the king of Goyim, and Amraphel the king of Shinar, and Arioch the king of Ellasar, four kings against the five.

Now the valley of Siddim was [composed of] many clay pits, and the kings of Sodom and Gomorrah fled and they fell there, and the survivors fled to a mountain.

And they took all the possessions of Sodom and Gomorrah and all their food, and they departed.

And they took Lot and his possessions, the son of Abram's brother, and they departed, and he was living in Sodom.

TEXT 1C

Ibid., 14–16

וַיִּשְׁמַע אַבְרָם כִּי נִשְׁבָּה אָחִיו וַיָּרֶק אֶת חֲנִיכָיו יְלִידֵי בֵיתוֹ שְׁמֹנָה עָשָׂר
וּשְׁלֹשׁ מֵאוֹת וַיִּרְדֹּף עַד דָּן:
וַיֵּחָלֵק עֲלֵיהֶם לַיְלָה הוּא וַעֲבָדָיו וַיַּכֵּם וַיִּרְדְּפֵם עַד חוֹבָה אֲשֶׁר
מִשְּׂמֹאל לְדַמָּשֶׂק:
וַיָּשֶׁב אֵת כָּל הָרְכֻשׁ וְגַם אֶת לוֹט אָחִיו וּרְכֻשׁוֹ הֵשִׁיב וְגַם אֶת הַנָּשִׁים
וְאֶת הָעָם:

And Abram heard that his kinsman had been taken captive, and he armed his trained men, those born in his house, three hundred and eighteen, and he pursued [them] until Dan.

And he divided himself against them at night, he and his servants, and smote them, and pursued them until Hobah, which is to the left of Damascus.

And he restored all the possessions, and also Lot his brother and his possessions he restored, and also the women and the people.

TEXT 1D

Ibid. 18–20

וּמַלְכִּי צֶדֶק מֶלֶךְ שָׁלֵם הוֹצִיא לֶחֶם וָיָיִן וְהוּא כֹהֵן לְקֵל עֶלְיוֹן:

וַיְבָרְכֵהוּ וַיֹּאמַר בָּרוּךְ אַבְרָם לְקֵל עֶלְיוֹן קֹנֵה שָׁמַיִם וָאָרֶץ:

וּבָרוּךְ קֵל עֶלְיוֹן אֲשֶׁר מִגֵּן צָרֶיךָ בְּיָדֶךָ וַיִּתֶּן לוֹ מַעֲשֵׂר מִכֹּל:

A nd Malkitzedek, the king of Salem, brought out bread and wine, and he was a priest to the Most High G-d.

And he blessed him, and he said, "Blessed be Abram to the Most High G-d, Who possesses heaven and earth.

"And blessed be the Most High G-d, Who has delivered your adversaries into your hand." And [Abram] gave [Malkitzedek] a tithe from all [of his property].

King Shem

TEXT 2A

Rabbi Shlomo Yitzchaki
(Rashi)
1040–1105
Most noted biblical and
Talmudic commentator.
Born in Troyes, France,
Rashi studied in the famed
yeshivot of Mainz and
Worms. His commentaries
on the Pentateuch and
the Talmud, which focus
on the straightforward
meaning of the text, appear
in virtually every edition
of the Talmud and Bible.

Rashi, Bereishit 14:18

"וּמַלְכִּי צֶדֶק." מִדְרַשׁ אַגָּדָה הוּא שֵׁם בֶּן נֹחַ.

"**A**nd Malkizedek." The Midrash Aggadah states that he was Shem, the son of Noah.

TEXT 2B

Rabbi Moshe ben Nachman
(Nachmanides, Ramban)
1194–1270
Scholar, philosopher, author
and physician. Nachmanides
was born in Spain and served
as leader of Iberian Jewry. In
1263, he was summoned by
King James of Aragon to a
public disputation with Pablo
Cristiani, a Jewish apostate.
Though Nachmanides was the
clear victor of the debate, he
had to flee Spain because of
the resulting persecution. He
moved to Israel and helped
reestablish communal life
in Jerusalem. He authored
a classic commentary
on the Pentateuch and a
commentary on the Talmud.

Nachmanides, Pirush Haramban, Bereishit, ad loc.

"וּמַלְכִּי צֶדֶק מֶלֶךְ שָׁלֵם." הִיא יְרוּשָׁלַיִם כָּעִנְיָן שֶׁנֶּאֱמַר "וַיְהִי בְשָׁלֵם סֻכּוֹ",
וּמַלְכָּהּ יִקָּרֵא גַם בִּימֵי יְהוֹשֻׁעַ "אֲדֹנִי צֶדֶק", כִּי מֵאָז יָדְעוּ הַגּוֹיִם כִּי הַמָּקוֹם
הַהוּא מֻבְחַר הַמְּקוֹמוֹת בְּאֶמְצַע הַיִּשּׁוּב אוֹ שֶׁיָּדְעוּ מַעֲלָתוֹ בְּקַבָּלָה שֶׁהוּא
מְכֻוָּן כְּנֶגֶד בֵּית הַמִּקְדָּשׁ שֶׁל מַעְלָה שֶׁשָּׁם שְׁכִינָתוֹ שֶׁל הַקָּדוֹשׁ בָּרוּךְ הוּא
שֶׁנִּקְרָא "צֶדֶק". וּבִבְרֵאשִׁית רַבָּה (מג ו) הַמָּקוֹם הַזֶּה מַצְדִּיק אֶת יוֹשְׁבָיו.
"וּמַלְכִּי צֶדֶק", אֲדֹנִי צֶדֶק נִקְרֵאת יְרוּשָׁלַם צֶדֶק, שֶׁנֶּאֱמַר (יְשַׁעְיָהוּ א כא)
"צֶדֶק יָלִין בָּהּ".

"**M**alkitzedek, king of Shalem." Shalem is Jerusalem, as the verse states, "His Tabernacle was in Shalem." Even years later, in the times of Joshua, the king of Shalem bore the title "Adonitzedek" ["Righteous Master"], for the nations already knew then that this place was the choicest place at the center of civilization... [The

Midrash] Bereishit Rabah states that this place makes its inhabitants righteous—for example, Malkitzedek, Adonitzedek. Jerusalem is called righteousness [tzedek] as the verse states, "In which righteousness would lodge."

Abraham's Mitzvah Observance

TEXT 3

Talmud Tractate Yoma, 28b

אמר רב קיים אברהם אבינו כל התורה כולה שנאמר עקב אשר שמע אברהם בקולי וגו׳.

av said: Abraham observed the entire Torah, as the verse states, "For Abraham listened to My voice…"

Babylonian Talmud

A literary work of monumental proportions that draws upon the legal, spiritual, intellectual, ethical, and historical traditions of Judaism. The 37 tractates of the Babylonian Talmud contain the teachings of the Jewish sages from the period after the destruction of the 2nd Temple through the 5th century CE. It has served as the primary vehicle for the transmission of the Oral Law and the education of Jews over the centuries; it is the entry point for all subsequent legal, ethical, and theological Jewish scholarship.

Laws of Ma'aser

Tithing Crops

TEXT 4A

Bamidbar (Numbers) 18:21

וְלִבְנֵי לֵוִי הִנֵּה נָתַתִּי כָּל מַעֲשֵׂר בְּיִשְׂרָאֵל לְנַחֲלָה חֵלֶף עֲבֹדָתָם אֲשֶׁר הֵם עֹבְדִים אֶת עֲבֹדַת אֹהֶל מוֹעֵד:

And to the descendants of Levi, I have given all tithes of Israel as an inheritance, in exchange for their service that they perform—the service of the Tent of Meeting.

TEXT 4B

Devarim (Deuteronomy) 14:22

עַשֵּׂר תְּעַשֵּׂר אֵת כָּל תְּבוּאַת זַרְעֶךָ הַיֹּצֵא הַשָּׂדֶה שָׁנָה שָׁנָה:

You shall tithe all the seed crop that the field gives forth, year by year.

TEXT 5

Rabbi Yosef Caro, Shulchan Aruch, Yoreh De'iah, 331:2

בזמן הזה... אין חיוב תרומות ומעשרות מן התורה אלא מדבריהם מפני שנאמר "כי תבואו"—משמע ביאת כולכם ולא ביאת מקצתן כמו שהיתה בימי עזרא.

In the current [post-Temple] era, the obligation to take terumot and ma'asrot is only of Rabbinic nature, for the verse states, "When you will come," i.e., when the entire Jewish people come to the land, not when only a portion of the people come, as was the case in the days of Ezra.

Rabbi Yosef Caro
(Maran, *Beit Yosef*)
1488– 1575
Halachic authority and author. Rabbi Caro was born in Spain, but was forced to flee during the expulsion in 1492 and eventually settled in Safed, Israel. He authored many works including the *Beit Yosef*, *Kesef Mishneh*, and a mystical work, *Magid Meisharim*. Rabbi Caro's magnum opus, the Shulchan Aruch (Code of Jewish Law), has been universally accepted as the basis for modern Jewish law.

Monetary Tithes

TEXT 6

Tosafot to Taanit 9a

"עשר תעשר." הכי איתא בסיפרי "עשר תעשר את כל תבואת זרעך היוצא השדה שנה שנה". אין לי אלא תבואת זרעך שחייב במעשר; רבית ופרקמטיא וכל שאר רווחים, מנין? תלמוד לומר "את כל", דהוה מצי למימר "את תבואתך"; מאי "כל"? – לרבות רבית ופרקמטיא וכל דבר שמרויח בו.

"You shall tithe." We have learned in Sifri: "You shall tithe all the seed crop that the field gives forth, year by year." This teaches only that we are obligated to tithe crops.

Tosafot
A collection of French and German Talmudic commentaries written during the 12th and 13th centuries. Among the most famous authors of *Tosafot* are Rabbi Ya'akov Tam, Rabbi Shimshon ben Abraham of Sens, and Rabbi Yitzchak ("the Ri"). Printed in almost all editions of the Talmud, these commentaries are fundamental to basic Talmudic study.

How do we know of the obligation to tithe interest, business, and all other types of profit?

*Instead of stating "the seed crop," the verse states, "**all** the seed crop." This teaches that interest, business, and all other earnings are included.*

TEXT 7

Rabbi Yitzchak Weiss, *Responsa Si'ach Yitzchak, ch. 457*

ואני תרתי בלבי מיד שרז"ל תיקנו מעשר כספים, כי היכא שלא תשתכח תורת מעשר מכל וכל בחוץ לארץ, וכדמצינו כמה פעמים 'שלא תשתכח תורת עירובין, ועיין פסחים (נא, ריש ע"א) "שלא תשתכח תורת חלה" עיין שם, ועיין סוכה (לא, ב), ועיין רש"י דפרשת קריאת שמע (דברים יא, יח דיבור המתחיל 'ושמתם את דברי') עשו ציונים לתורה שלא יהיה חדשות לעתיד.

Our Sages instituted monetary tithing so the idea of tithing should not be completely forgotten in the Diaspora. We find parallels to this idea, with the Sages instituting decrees so as not to forget the concept of eruvin, challah, *etc. Cf. Rashi* in the parashah *of* Shema, *"Even after you have been exiled, make yourselves distinctive with My commandments … so that these will not be new to you when you return."*

When, What, and How

TEXT 8A

Rabbi Yechiel Michel Epstein, Aruch Hashulchan, Yoreh Dei'ah 249:7

וכן הוא דבר פשוט שהריוח מחשבין בכל שנה ושנה מראש הנה עד
ראש הנה ואם בשנה זו היו לו עסקים שיש שהרויח בהם ויש שהפסיד
בהם עושה חשבון כללי ומה שנשאר ריוח נותן מעשר לצדקה.

I t makes sense that profits are calculated every
year from Rosh Hashanah to Rosh Hashanah. If
in the past year one had business incurring some
profits and some losses, he makes one general calculation, and gives ten percent of the overall profit.

Rabbi Yechiel Michel Halevi Epstein
1829–1908
Noted author on Jewish law. Rabbi Epstein lived in Czarist Lithuania and was chief rabbi of Novozypkov, a town near Minsk, and later, of Navahrudak, where he served until his death. A prolific writer, his primary work is *Aruch Hashulchan*, an expanded and reworked code of Jewish law.

TEXT 8B

Ibid.

—ובכלל ריוח נחשב רק הריוח הנקי וכל ההוצאות שהיה לו על העסק
אף מה שנסע הוא בדרך ואכל ושתה—הכל נחשב על הוצאות העסק,
ומנכה הכל, ומה שנשאר ריוח אחר ניכוי כל ההוצאות מקרי ריוח. אבל
הוצאות ביתו לא ינכה ולכן מי שמרויח אלף זהובים לשנה נותן מאה או
מאתים לצדקה אע"ג שהוא בעל הוצאה בביתו עוד יותר מאלף זהובים
מ"מ חייב ליתן מעשר מהריוח ורק מה שהיה צדקה בההוצאה כגון
שחלק לחם בב' וה' או נתן פרוטות לעניים או נתן לאכול איזה יום לבני
ת"ת או לקח אורח עני על על שבת או על סעודה ביום כדרך בני ישראל
יכול לנכות מחלק המעשר.

Only actual profit is counted. Any business expenses, such as travel and dining expenses, can be subtracted from the total; only the remainder is considered profit.

Personal expenses, however, may not be deducted. Therefore, if one made a thousand gold coins in a year, he gives 100 (or 200) to charity. Even if he spent more than a thousand gold coins on his personal expenses, he must nevertheless give ten percent of his profits.

However, charity expenses such as providing food and funds to the poor, feeding the children of Torah scholars, or hosting a poor guest for the Shabbat meal or any other day meal as is the Jewish way—such funds may be deducted from the ma'aser calculation.

TEXT 9

Rabbi Moshe Feinstein
1895–1986
Leading halachic authority of the 20th century. Rabbi Feinstein was appointed rabbi of Luban, Belarus, in 1921. He immigrated to the U.S. in 1937 and became the dean of Metivta Tiferet Yerushalayim in New York. Rabbi Feinstein's halachic decisions have been published in a multivolume collection entitled *Igrot Moshe*.

Rabbi Moshe Feinstein, Igrot Moshe, Yoreh Dei'ah Part 1, §143

ואם רוצה להדר ולהחמיר לעשר מכל ריוח ביחוד ודאי הוא משובח.

It is certainly praiseworthy to be stringent and tithe each and every profit individually.

Give and Get

TEXT 10A

Talmud Tractate Ta'anit, 9a

אמר רבי יוחנן מאי דכתיב "עשר תעשר"? –עשר בשביל שתתעשר.

Rabbi Yochanan said, what is the meaning of the verse "עשר תעשר", ["You shall tithe," using a double term]? Tithe ("עשר" with a sin) so that you will prosper ("תתעשר" with a shin, which means "to become wealthy").

Babylonian Talmud
A literary work of monumental proportions that draws upon the legal, spiritual, intellectual, ethical, and historical traditions of Judaism. The 37 tractates of the Babylonian Talmud contain the teachings of the Jewish sages from the period after the destruction of the 2nd Temple through the 5th century CE. It has served as the primary vehicle for the transmission of the Oral Law and the education of Jews over the centuries; it is the entry point for all subsequent legal, ethical, and theological Jewish scholarship.

TEXT 10B

Malachi 3:10

הָבִיאוּ אֶת כָּל הַמַּעֲשֵׂר אֶל בֵּית הָאוֹצָר וִיהִי טֶרֶף בְּבֵיתִי וּבְחָנוּנִי נָא בָּזֹאת אָמַר ה' צְבָאוֹת אִם לֹא אֶפְתַּח לָכֶם אֵת אֲרֻבּוֹת הַשָּׁמַיִם וַהֲרִיקֹתִי לָכֶם בְּרָכָה עַד בְּלִי דָי:

Bring the whole of the tithes into the treasury so that there may be nourishment in My House, and **test Me now therewith**, says the Lord of Hosts, [to see] if I will not open for you the sluices of heaven and pour down for you blessing until there be no room to suffice for it.

TEXT 10C

Rabbi Menachem Mendel Schneerson
1902–1994

The towering Jewish leader of the 20th century, known as "the Lubavitcher Rebbe," or simply as "the Rebbe." Born in southern Ukraine, the Rebbe escaped Nazi-occupied Europe, arriving in the U.S. in June 1941. The Rebbe inspired and guided the revival of traditional Judaism after the European devastation, impacting virtually every Jewish community the world over. The Rebbe often emphasized that the performance of just one additional good deed could usher in the era of Moshiach. The Rebbe's scholarly talks and writings have been printed in more than 200 volumes.

The Lubavitcher Rebbe, Torat Menachem Hitva'aduyot, vol. 21, p. 234–5

בכלל הסדר שלי שאיני מתערב להביע דעתי בנוגע לכמות הנתינה של כל אחד; הנני לוקח את הנתינה, ואחד מן השנים: או שהנני מרוצה, או שאיני מרוצה, ומשאיר את העדר שביעת הרצון לעצמי. אך כיון שזהו לגמרי ענין היוצא מן הכלל, אהיה גם אני יוצא מן הגדר ויוצא מן הכלל, ואם יהיה נראה בעיני שנותנים סכום פחות מדי)"צו וייניק" (אסיר את מסוה הבושה ("איך וועל זיך אפשעמען"), ואצוה עליו—בכח העניינים שעבורם צריכים את הכסף (ובנדון דידן: השיכון)—להוסיף כפי שיראה בעיני.

ובטוחני שהקדוש ברוך הוא יעמוד בדיבורו—שאמר "עשר בשביל שתתעשר", ואמר "ובחנוני נא בזאת...והריקותי לכם ברכה עד בלי די"... ואם יהיה נראה למישהו שציוו עליו לתת סכום שלא לפי כחו—הנה הכוונה בזה היא כדי שהקדוש ברוך הוא יתן לו לכל-הפחות ארבעה פעמים, ובמילא, כשיוסיף עוד אלף דולר, יתן לו הקדוש ברוך הוא עוד ארבעת אלפים דולר!

In general, I don't voice my opinion as to how much each person gives; I accept the donation, and one of two things happens: Either I am satisfied, or if I am not satisfied, I keep my dissatisfaction to myself.

But as this is something out of the ordinary, I too will not keep my regular habit. If I feel someone has donated too little, I will overcome my shyness and tell him—in accordance with the importance of this project (the housing in Kfar Chabad) to increase the amount as I see fit...

I am certain that G-d will keep His word, "Tithe so that you will prosper," and "Test Me now therewith… I will pour down for you blessing until there be no room to suffice for it."… If one feels that he has been asked to give more than he can afford, the purpose is so that G-d will reimburse him at least four-fold. So if he increases his donation by $1,000, G-d will give him an additional four thousand!

STORY

Standing in the crowd that night was the *chasid* Reb Dovid Deitsch, of New Haven, CT. He was by no means very wealthy at the time, but was an extremely generous person. When donation slips were passed around the *farbrengen*, he put down a pledge of $3,000. In those days, that was an incredibly large sum for someone in his position (worth about $25,000 today), and he did not imagine the Rebbe would add anything to it. Yet seeing his card, the Rebbe announced, "Dovid Deitsch: Ten times this amount!"

Reb Dovid had absolutely no clue how he could come up with such a sum (a quarter of a million in today's dollars), but as a true *chasid*, he returned home with faith that all would work out.

Driving back into New Haven the next day, he was surprised to spot a banker he knew walking in the street. Recognizing his opportunity, he rolled down his window and decided to ask for a $30,000 loan. Needless to say, the banker was hesitant to lend such an exorbitant amount to a person not known for his great wealth. After Reb Dovid put his home, his business, and his good name on the line, the banker acquiesced. Reb Dovid returned to Crown Heights with a check.

A short while later, he received a call from a vinyl supplier up in Boston. "Dave," the man said, "We've had a warehouse fire, and we've got loads of slightly damaged vinyl. We're trying to get rid of it all so we can start from scratch. Would you buy it at a heavy discount?"

Reb Dovid, who dealt in small pieces of vinyl, agreed. After buying a large amount and seeing it sell quickly at triple the usual profit, he returned to Boston with the largest tractor trailer he could find and loaded up the rest of the material. When all was said and done, he had made a profit beyond his wildest imagination.

At this point, he returned to Crown Heights to give a check to the Rebbe's secretariat for an additional $30,000. The Rebbe sent the check back with the message that should Reb Dovid agree, he'd like to be his new business partner. Reb Dovid happily agreed and from then on, his business prospered, making him a very wealthy and charitable man, remembered today as the "father of Oholei Torah," Chabad's flagship boys' school and *yeshivah* in Crown Heights.

The Meaning of Ma'aser

Everything Belongs to G-d

TEXT 11

Rabbi Aharon Halevi of Barcelona. Sefer Hachinuch, §18

משרשי מצוה זו שרצה השם יתברך לזכתנו לעשות מצוה בראשית
פריו, למען דעת כי הכל שלו, ואין לו לאדם דבר בעולם רק מה שיחלק
לנו השם יתברך בחסדיו. ויבין זה בראותו, כי אחר שיגע האדם כמה
יגיעות וטרח כמה טורחים בעולמו, והגיע לזמן שעשה פרי, וחביב עליו
ראשית פריו כבבת עינו—מיד נותנו להקדוש ברוך הוא ומתרוקן רשותו
ממנו ומכניסו לרשות בוראו.

Rabbi Aharon Halevi of Barcelona
(Re'ah)
1235–1290
Born in Gerona, Spain. Rabbi, talmudist, and authority on Jewish law. Rabbi Aharon studied under Nachmanides and under his father, Rabbi Yosef Halevi, and corresponded with the leading talmudic scholars of his generation. His explanations on the Rashba's halachic code, *Torat Habayit*, entitled *Bedek Habayit*, are integral in the formation of Jewish law. Rabbi Aharon was considered by some to be the anonymous author of *Sefer Hachinuch*, a compendium of the 613 commandments.

The reasons for this mitzvah: G-d wished to give us the privilege of doing a mitzvah with the first of our fruit. In this way we know that everything belongs to Him, and that Man owns nothing in this world apart from what G-d bestows upon him in His great kindness. After one has toiled laboriously, and can now see the fruits of his labor that are dear to him as the apple of his eye, and then immediately gives it to G-d and relinquishes his ownership, it impresses upon him that everything is in the domain of his Creator.

TEXT 12

The Lubavitcher Rebbe, Likutei Sichot, vol. 5 p. 70

די אלגעמיינע באדייטונג פון מצות מעשר וואס מען דארף געבן צום
לוי (און על דרך זה מעשר כספים וואס מען דארף געבן אויף צדקה)
איז—"לה' הארץ ומלואה", אז אלץ וואס א איד פארמאגט געהערט
צום אויבערשטן, און דעריבער דארף ער צום אלעם ערשטן אפגעבן א
צענטל—און דער צענטל דארף זיין מן המובחר—צום לוי וואס "הוי'
הוא נחלתו", און ערשט נאך דעם, נוצט ער די אנדערע טיילן פאר זיינע
אייגעניע צוועקן.

The conventional significance of the obligation to give ten percent to a Levite (as well as the obligation to give monetary ma'aser to charity) is—"The land and the fullness thereof are G-d's," that everything a Jew has belongs to G-d. Therefore, a Jew must first of all give a tenth—of the best of his crop—to a Levite, of whom it states, "G-d is his inheritance." Only then may he use the remainder for his personal needs.

Two Types of Mitzvot

TEXT 13

Maimonides, Mishneh Torah, Laws of Bechorot, 1:1

מצות עשה להפריש כל פטר רחם הזכרים בין באדם בין בבהמה טהורה בין ממין החמור בין שהיו שלימים בין שהיו טריפות שנאמר קדש לי כל בכור פטר כל רחם בבני ישראל באדם ובבהמה וכולן לכהנים.

I t is a positive commandment to set aside all the male firstborn of the womb, whether among humans, kosher animals, and donkeys. This applies whether the animals are healthy or treifot. Thus, the verse states, "Consecrate unto Me all firstborn, the first issue of the womb among the Children of Israel, in humans and in animals." All of the above are given to the priests.

Rabbi Moshe ben Maimon (Maimonides, Rambam) 1135–1204

Halachist, philosopher, author, and physician. Maimonides was born in Cordoba, Spain. After the conquest of Cordoba by the Almohads, he fled Spain and eventually settled in Cairo, Egypt. There, he became the leader of the Jewish community and served as court physician to the vizier of Egypt. He is most noted for authoring the *Mishneh Torah*, an encyclopedic arrangement of Jewish law, and for his philosophical work, *Guide for the Perplexed*. His rulings on Jewish law are integral to the formation of halachic consensus.

TEXT 14

Maimonides, Mishneh Torah, Laws of Bikurim, 2:1

מצות עשה להביא בכורים למקדש ואינם נוהגין אלא בפני הבית ובארץ
ישראל בלבד שנאמר ראשית בכורי אדמתך תביא בית ה' אלקיך.

It is a positive commandment to bring the first fruits to the Temple. The obligation of the first fruits applies only while the Temple is standing, and only in Israel, as [implied by the verse,] "Bring of the first ripened fruit of your land to the house of G-d your Lord."

A Set Amount

TEXT 15

Maimonides, Ibid. 2:17

הבכורים אין להם שיעור מן התורה אבל מדבריהם צריך להפריש אחד
מששים והרוצה לעשות כל שדהו בכורים עושהו.

There is no set measure for the first fruits according to Scriptural law. According to Rabbinic law, one should give one-sixtieth of the crop. If one desires to set aside his entire crop as first fruits, he may.

TEXT 16

Maimonides, Mishneh Torah, Laws of Ma'asrot, 1:1

אחר שמפרישין תרומה גדולה מפריש אחד מעשרה מן הנשאר וזהו
הנקרא מעשר ראשון ובו נאמר כי את מעשר בני ישראל אשר ירימו
ליי' וגו' והמעשר הזה ללויים זכרים ונקבות שנאמר ולבני לוי הנה נתתי
כל מעשר בישראל לנחלה.

After separating terumah, *one should separate one-tenth of the remaining produce and this is called the first tithe. Concerning it, the verse states, "For the tithes of the Children of Israel that they will separate to G-d."*

TEXT 17A

Likutei Sichot, vol 21. p. 71

פון דעם איז מובן אז אין מצות מעשר ווערט ספעציעל אונטערשטראכן
דער געדאנק פון "לה' הארץ ומלואה" מער ווי אין מתנות כהונה: אז
דעם אויבערשטנס בעל-הבית'שקייט איז אויף דעם אייגנטום
וואס געהערט לכאורה אינגאנצן צום מענשן, און דאס—אין דער
צייט ווען עו געהערט צום מענטשן (קודח ההפרשה); און ניט בלויז אן
אלגעמיינע בעה"ב'שקייט (אזוי ווי ביי תרומה אין דאס גליכן), נאר—
באופן קבוע ומדוד.

The mitzvah of ma'aser *uniquely empha- sizes the notion that "the land and the fullness thereof are G-d's," more so than other priestly* gifts. Ma'aser *indicates that G-d's ownership extends* *even to one's personal property, that seemingly belong entirely to him—at the very time that it still belongs to him (i.e., before he separates ten percent); and not in a general way (as is the case with* terumah *and the like), but in a set and measured way.*

STORY

Rabbi Binyamin Kletzker, one of the greatest *chasidim* of the Alter Rebbe, was a lumber merchant by trade. Once, while adding up his profits, he inadvertently wrote as his total, *"Ein od milvado"*—there is nothing other than G-d.

A G-dly Purpose in Everything

TEXT 17B

Likutei Sichot, Ibid., p. 76

מצות מעשר באדייט דאך אז אויך דעם מענטשנס פריוואטע ענינים
וועלכע ער טוט מצד טבעו... דארפן זיי זיין דורכגעדרונגען מיט אלקות
(וכמובן בפשטות פון דעם וואס פון יעדער רכוש וואס א איד האט,
אויך ווען ער איז אויסן די "גשמיות" דערפון, דארף ער געבן דערפון א
צענטל צום אויבערשטן), דארף מען דעריבער נעמען דעם כח דערויף
פון אברהם'ען וואס האט געגעבן מעשר פון א רכוש וואס "ענינו"
איז "גשמיות."

Ma'aser *means that even one's private affairs
that he does by habit … need to be satu-
rated with G-dliness (as is understood from
the fact that a Jew must tithe everything he owns, and
even the very corporeal aspects thereof).*

3

Sorry, No Shortcuts Here

Personal Investment in Judaism

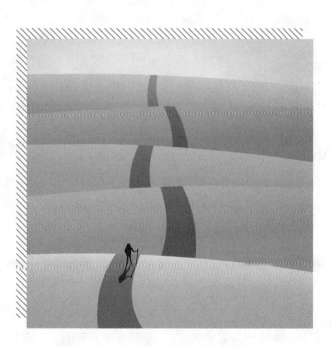

Dedicated in loving memory of Susan Moses on the occasion of her yahrtzeit, 16 Cheshvan

לע"נ זמירה לאה בת צבי הלוי

PARASHA OVERVIEW
Vayera

G-d reveals Himself to Abraham three days after the first Jew's circumcision at age ninety-nine; but Abraham rushes off to prepare a meal for three guests who appear in the desert heat. One of the three—who are angels disguised as men—announces that, in exactly one year, the barren Sarah will give birth to a son. Sarah laughs.

Abraham pleads with G-d to spare the wicked city of Sodom. Two of the three disguised angels arrive in the doomed city, where Abraham's nephew Lot extends his hospitality to them and protects them from the evil intentions of a Sodomite mob. The two guests reveal that they have come to overturn the place, and to save Lot and his family. Lot's wife turns into a pillar of salt when she disobeys the command not to look back at the burning city as they flee.

While taking shelter in a cave, Lot's two daughters (believing that they and their father are the only ones left alive in the world) get their father drunk, lie with him and become pregnant. The two sons born from this incident father the nations of Moab and Ammon.

Abraham moves to Gerar, where the Philistine king Abimelech takes Sarah—who is presented as Abraham's sister—to his palace. In a dream, G-d warns Abimelech that he will die unless he returns the woman to her husband. Abraham explains that he feared he would be killed over the beautiful Sarah.

G-d remembers His promise to Sarah, and gives her and Abraham a son, who is named Isaac (Yitzchak, meaning "will laugh"). Isaac is circumcised at the age of eight days; Abraham is one hundred years old, and Sarah ninety, at their child's birth.

Hagar and Ishmael are banished from Abraham's home and wander in the desert; G-d hears the cry of the dying lad, and saves his life by showing his mother a well. Abimelech makes a treaty with Abraham at Beersheba, where Abraham gives him seven sheep as a sign of their truce.

G-d tests Abraham's devotion by commanding him to sacrifice Isaac on Mount Moriah (the Temple Mount) in Jerusalem. Isaac is bound and placed on the altar, and Abraham raises the knife to slaughter his son. A voice from heaven calls to stop him; a ram, caught in the undergrowth by its horns, is offered in Isaac's place. Abraham receives the news of the birth of a daughter, Rebecca, to his nephew Bethuel.

Guest of Honor

All day long, Berel would shuffle around, not bothering to do anything productive. One year, on the first night of Chanukah, his wife tried to put him to work. She asked him to get a carton of eggs from the market so she could make *latkes,* as European Jews do. After a bit of cajoling, off he went.

On his way to the market, he encountered a wagon full of his fellow Chasidim getting ready to embark on a journey. "Where are you off to?" he asked. Eagerly, they replied, "We are going to be with the Rebbe for the first night of Chanukah! We'll light the menorah, *farbreng,* and make a few *l'chaims*!" Caught up in the excitement, it didn't take more than a moment for Berel to forget his wife, his family, and his errand. He excitedly jumped on board and joined the group.

Chanukah with the Rebbe was truly wonderful. Each evening after candle lighting, the Rebbe spoke uplifting words of Torah, and the Chasidim *farbrenged* and rejoiced. The days passed quickly and Berel enjoyed every minute. On the last day of Chanukah, it all came crashing back to him. *"Oy vey!"* he cried. "My poor wife is waiting at home all alone for me to bring back the carton of eggs she asked for." Hysterical, he jumped on the first available wagon and rushed back to town. Upon arriving, he quickly ran to the market and purchased the eggs, before running home, exhausted and out of breath. Upon crossing the threshold of his house, he lost his balance, and was horrified to see every last egg come crashing to the ground.

"You see, Rochel," he exclaimed, "haste makes waste..."

Avraham's Enthusiasm

TEXT 1A

Bereishit (Genesis) 18:2

וַיִּשָּׂא עֵינָיו וַיַּרְא וְהִנֵּה שְׁלֹשָׁה אֲנָשִׁים נִצָּבִים עָלָיו וַיַּרְא וַיָּרָץ לִקְרָאתָם מִפֶּתַח הָאֹהֶל וַיִּשְׁתַּחוּ אָרְצָה:

And he lifted his eyes and saw, and behold, three men were standing beside him, and he saw and he ran toward them from the entrance of the tent, and he prostrated himself to the ground.

TEXT 1B

Ibid., 6–7

וַיְמַהֵר אַבְרָהָם הָאֹהֱלָה אֶל שָׂרָה וַיֹּאמֶר מַהֲרִי שְׁלֹשׁ סְאִים קֶמַח סֹלֶת לוּשִׁי וַעֲשִׂי עֻגוֹת:
וְאֶל הַבָּקָר רָץ אַבְרָהָם וַיִּקַּח בֶּן בָּקָר רַךְ וָטוֹב וַיִּתֵּן אֶל הַנַּעַר וַיְמַהֵר לַעֲשׂוֹת אֹתוֹ:

And Abraham hastened to the tent to Sarah, and he said, "Hasten three se'ah of meal and fine flour; knead and make cakes."

And to the cattle did Abraham run, and he took a calf, tender and good, and he gave it to the youth, and he hastened to prepare it.

TEXT 2A

Ibid., 22:3

וַיַּשְׁכֵּם אַבְרָהָם בַּבֹּקֶר וַיַּחֲבֹשׁ אֶת חֲמֹרוֹ וַיִּקַּח אֶת שְׁנֵי נְעָרָיו אִתּוֹ וְאֵת יִצְחָק בְּנוֹ וַיְבַקַּע עֲצֵי עֹלָה וַיָּקָם וַיֵּלֶךְ אֶל הַמָּקוֹם אֲשֶׁר אָמַר לוֹ הָאֱלֹקִים.

And Abraham arose early in the morning, and he saddled his donkey, and he took his two young men with him and Isaac his son; and he split wood for a burnt offering, and he arose and went to the place of which G-d had told him.

TEXT 2B

Talmud Tractate Pesachim, 4a

Babylonian Talmud
A literary work of monumental proportions that draws upon the legal, spiritual, intellectual, ethical, and historical traditions of Judaism. The 37 tractates of the Babylonian Talmud contain the teachings of the Jewish sages from the period after the destruction of the 2nd Temple through the 5th century CE. It has served as the primary vehicle for the transmission of the Oral Law and the education of Jews over the centuries; it is the entry point for all subsequent legal, ethical, and theological Jewish scholarship.

כל היום כשר למילה, אלא שזריזים מקדימים למצוות. שנאמר: וישכם אברהם בבוקה.

A brit milah *may be performed all day long,* but "the eager perform mitzvot *early*," as the verse states, "And Abraham arose early in the morning."

A Strange Visit

TEXT 3A

Bereishit (Genesis) 18:1

וַיֵּרָא אֵלָיו ה' בְּאֵלֹנֵי מַמְרֵא וְהוּא יֹשֵׁב פֶּתַח הָאֹהֶל כְּחֹם הַיּוֹם:

-d appeared to him in the plains of Mamre, and he was sitting at the entrance of the tent when the day was hot.

TEXT 3B

Ibid., v. 2

וַיִּשָּׂא עֵינָיו וַיַּרְא וְהִנֵּה שְׁלֹשָׁה אֲנָשִׁים נִצָּבִים עָלָיו וַיַּרְא וַיָּרָץ לִקְרָאתָם מִפֶּתַח הָאֹהֶל וַיִּשְׁתַּחוּ אָרְצָה:

And he lifted his eyes and saw, and behold, three men were standing beside him, and he saw and he ran toward them from the entrance of the tent, and he prostrated himself to the ground.

TEXT 3C

Talmud Tractate Baba Metzia, 86b

אותו היום יום שלישי של מילה של אברהם היה ובא הקדוש ברוך הוא לשאול באברהם.

I t was the third day from Abraham's circumcision, and G-d came to see how he was doing.

TEXT 4

Rabbi Asher ben Yechiel
(Rosh)
1250–1328
Rabbi, author, and Talmudist, he is widely known by the acronym "Rosh." Rabbi Asher was a native of Germany, where he was a prominent disciple and successor of Rabbi Meir ("the Maharam") of Rothenburg. Due to the persecution and massacres of German Jewry under Emperor Rudolph I, Rabbi Asher was forced to flee, and in 1305, he arrived in Toledo, Spain.
He is best known for his halachic commentary on the Talmud. Rabbi Asher was the father of Rabbi Ya'akov, the author of the *Arba'ah Turim*.

Tosafot Harosh, ad loc.

וירא אליו – לבקר את החולה ... ובא ללמד דרך ארץ שיש לו לאדם לבקר החולה ואפילו לא ידבר עמו דבר. כגון שמצאו ישן, דניחא לחולה כשיגידו לו שפלוני בא לראותו.

"G -d appeared to him." To visit the sick… this teaches that it is appropriate to visit a sick person, even if there is no opportunity to talk with him. For example, if the patient is sleeping, it still helps him to know after the fact that so-and-so came to visit him.

Question—Why Wait?

TEXT 5

The Lubavitcher Rebbe, Likutei Sichot, vol. 5, p. 77

השאלה גדולה יותר: למה הקדוש ברוך הוא המתין עם ביקור החולה
עד היום השלישי ולא הגיע לבקר את החולה קודם?

he big question here is: Why did G-d wait until the third day to visit him? Why didn't He come right away?

Rabbi Menachem Mendel Schneerson
1902–1994

The towering Jewish leader of the 20th century, known as "the Lubavitcher Rebbe," or simply as "the Rebbe." Born in southern Ukraine, the Rebbe escaped Nazi-occupied Europe, arriving in the U.S. in June 1941. The Rebbe inspired and guided the revival of traditional Judaism after the European devastation, impacting virtually every Jewish community the world over. The Rebbe often emphasized that the performance of just one additional good deed could usher in the era of Moshiach. The Rebbe's scholarly talks and writings have been printed in more than 200 volumes.

The Power to Heal

G-dly Behavior

TEXT 6

Shemot Rabah

An early rabbinic commentary on the Book of Exodus. Midrash is the designation of a particular genre of rabbinic literature usually forming a running commentary on specific books of the Bible.

Shemot Rabah, written mostly in Hebrew, provides textual exegeses, expounds upon the biblical narrative, and develops and illustrates moral principles. It was first printed in Constantinople in 1512 together with four other midrashic works on the other four books of the Pentateuch.

Midrash Shemot Rabah, 30:9

מגיד דבריו ליעקב חוקיו ומשפטיו לישראל—לפי שאין מידותיו של הקדוש ברוך הוא כמידת בשר ודם. מידת בשר ודם, מורה לאחרים לעשות, והוא אינו עושה כלום. והקדוש ברוך הוא, מה שהוא עושה, אומר הוא לישראל לעשות ולשמור.

"He tells His words to Jacob, His statutes and His judgments to Israel." G-d is unlike man—man commands others to do, but himself does nothing; but G-d—what He does, He tells the Jewish people to do and keep.

TEXT 7

Talmud Tractate Sotah, 14a

"אחרי ה' אלהיכם תלכו"—וכי אפשר להלך אחר שכינה? והלוא נאמר "כי ה' אלהיך אש אוכלה הוא"? אלא להלך אחר מדותיו של הקדוש ברוך הוא... ה' ביקר חולים, דכתיב ו"ירא אליו ה' באלוני ממרא", אף אתה בקר חולים.

The verse states, "You will go after G-d." But is it possible to go after Him? Does it not say, "The Lord your G-d is a consuming fire"?

Rather, it means you should follow G-d's ways… G-d visited the sick, as it says, "G-d appeared to him in the plains of Mamre," so should you visit the sick.

A Great Reward

TEXT 8A

Talmud Tractate Nedarim, 40a

כל המבקר את החולה – מה שכרו? ניצול מדינה של גהנום. ומה שכרו בעולם הזה? "ה' ישמרהו ויחיהו ואשר בארץ ואל תתנהו בנפש איביו". כלומר: ה' ישמרהו – מיצר הרע. ויחיהו – מן היסורין. ואשר בארץ – שיהו הכל מתכבדים בו. ואל תתנהו בנפש איביו – שיזדמנו לו רעים כנעמן שריפאו את צרעתו.

What is the reward for one who visits the sick? He is saved from purgatory. And what is his reward in this world? "G-d will preserve him and keep him alive, and he will be praised in the land, and You will not deliver him into the desire of his enemies."

"G-d will preserve him"—from the evil inclination.

"And keep him alive"—from suffering.

"And he will be praised on the land"—all will take pride in him.

"And You will not deliver him into the desire of his enemies"—G-d will give him friends like Naaman's friends, who cured his leprosy.

Giving the Gift of Life

TEXT 8B

Ibid.

רב דימי אמר: כל המבקר את החולה גורם לו שיחיה וכל שאינו מבקר גורם לו שימות.

av Dimi said: Anyone who visits a sick person causes him to live. Anyone who does not visit causes him to die.

TEXT 8C

Nachmanides, Torat Ha'adam, Sha'ar Hamichush

ביקור חולים הוא כדי שיכבדו וירבצו לפניו [ינקו את החדר ויסדרו] ויעשו לו צרכים הצריכים לחוליו וימצא נחת רוח עם חבריו.

The purpose of visiting the sick is so that the patient's room will be swept and cleaned, all his needs will be tended to, and the patient will be calmed by his friends.

Rabbi Moshe ben Nachman
(Nachmanides, Ramban)
1194–1270
Scholar, philosopher, author and physician. Nachmanides was born in Spain and served as leader of Iberian Jewry. In 1263, he was summoned by King James of Aragon to a public disputation with Pablo Cristiani, a Jewish apostate. Though Nachmanides was the clear victor of the debate, he had to flee Spain because of the resulting persecution. He moved to Israel and helped reestablish communal life in Jerusalem. He authored a classic commentary on the Pentateuch and a commentary on the Talmud.

TEXT 8D

Talmud Tractate Nedarim, 40a

לא כך היה מעשה בתלמיד אחד מתלמידי רבי עקיבא שחלה, לא נכנסו חכמים לבקרו, ונכנס רבי עקיבא לבקרו, ובשביל שכיבדו וריבצו לפניו חיה. אמר לו: רבי, החייתני. יצא רבי עקיבא ודרש: כל מי שאין מבקר חולים, כאילו שופך דמים!

Once, a student of Rabbi Akiva fell ill, and the Sages did not visit him. Rabbi Akiva did go to visit him, and because he swept and cleaned the premises, the patient lived. He said to Rabbi Akiva, "You have given me life!"

Rabbi Akiva left and said, "Anyone who does not visit the sick is considered to have murdered!"

TEXT 9

Rabbi Yosef Caro
(Maran, *Beit Yosef*)
1488– 1575

Halachic authority and author. Rabbi Caro was born in Spain, but was forced to flee during the expulsion in 1492 and eventually settled in Safed, Israel. He authored many works including the *Beit Yosef*, *Kesef Mishneh*, and a mystical work, *Magid Meisharim*. Rabbi Caro's magnum opus, the Shulchan Aruch (Code of Jewish Law), has been universally accepted as the basis for modern Jewish law.

Rabbi Yosef Caro, Shulchan Aruch, Yoreh Dei'ah, 335:4–6

אין מבקרים את החולה בשלוש שעות ראשונות של היום, מפני שכל חולה מיקל עליו חליו בבוקר ולא יחוש לבקש עליו רחמים. ולא בשלוש שעות אחרונות של היום שאז מכביד עליו החולי ויתייאש מלבקש עליו רחמים. רמ"א: וכל שביקר ולא ביקש עליו רחמים לא קיים המצווה. כשמבקש עליו רחמים... יכלול אותו בתוך שאר חולי ישראל ויאמר: המקום ירחם עליך בתוך חולי ישראל.

One should not visit the sick in the first three hours of the day, because a patient's condition is better in the morning, and therefore the visitor will not be moved to pray for him.

Nor should one visit in the last three hours of the day, for then the patient's sickness is more severe, and the visitor will lose hope and see no reason to pray for him.

Note of the Rema: One who visits but does not pray for the patient has not fulfilled the mitzvah of visiting the sick.

When praying, one should include the patient among all the sick people of Israel and say, "May G-d have mercy on you, together with all the sick people of Israel."

Remote Bikur Cholim

TEXT 10A

Rabbi Yitzchak Hutner, Pachad Yitzchak,
Letters and Writings, Letter 33

נראה כי תרגומה של המילה "ביקור" אינו מלשון "וויזיט", אלא מלשון
"ביקורת תהיה", כלומר העיון במצבו של החולה... ובמובן זה של ביקור
חולים אין הבדל יסודי בין שיחת טלפון או התעסקות באופן אחר.

I would suggest that the word "*ביקור*" does not mean "visit," but "inquiry," as in the verse "*ביקורת תהיה*," i.e., an inquiry into the patient's condition… In this sense, there's no real difference whether the mitzvah is performed via telephone call or by helping the patient out in some other way.

TEXT 10B

Rabbi Moshe Feinstein, Igrot Moshe, Yoreh Deiah Part One, §223

בדבר ביקור חולים על ידי שאלה בטלפון, אף שכל העניינים שכתבו
הטור והבית יוסף בשם הרמב"ן [לבקש עליו רחמים] אינו מקיים... [לכן]
פשוט לעניות דעתי שאף שמקיים מצווה דביקור חולים [משום עצם
ההתעניינות במצבו], אבל אין שייך לומר שיצא ידי חובה [כל צרכו],
כיון שחסר בביקור זה העניינים האחרים דביקור חולים [התפילה עליו].

As for fulfilling bikur cholim *by way of a telephone call: This does not fulfill all the aspects of the mitzvah stated by the* Tur *and*

Rabbi Moshe Feinstein
1895–1986

Leading halachic authority of the 20th century, Rabbi Feinstein was appointed rabbi of Luban, Belarus, in 1921. He immigrated to the U.S. in 1937 and became the dean of Metivta Tiferet Yerushalayim in New York. Rabbi Feinstein's halachic decisions have been published in a multivolume collection entitled *Igrot Moshe.*

the Beit Yosef *in the name of the Ramban [i.e., being motivated to pray on the patient's behalf]. Therefore, it is clear that although one fulfills the mitzvah to some extent [by showing interest in the patient's condition], he has not totally fulfilled the obligation, because the other aspects of* bikur cholim *[namely, praying on the patient's behalf] are lacking.*

Why G-d Waited

People Speak

TEXT 11

Talmud Tractate Nedarim, 40a

רבא, יומא קדמאה דחליש אמר להון: לא תיגלו לאיניש, דלא לתרע
מזליה (דדילמא מתצלנא לאלתר, אי נמי דלא לישתעי מילי עילויה. —
רש"י). מכאן ואילך אמר להון: פוקו ואכריזו בשוקא, דכל דסני לי ליחדי
לי, וכתיב: בנפול אויבך אל תשמח וגו', ודרחים לי ליבעי עלי רחמי.

Rava fell ill. On the first day of his illness, he requested that the matter not be made public, so as not to negatively affect his mazal. Henceforth, he asked them to announce his illness in the marketplace. He reasoned, "Anyone who hates me will rejoice—and it is written, 'You shall not rejoice in the fall of your enemy, etc.' Conversely, anyone who loves me will pray on my behalf."

TEXT 12

Rabbi Chayim ibn Atar
(*Or Hachayim*)
1696–1743
Biblical exegete, Kabbalist, and Talmudist. Rabbi Atar, born in Meknes, Morocco, was a prominent member of the Moroccan rabbinate and later immigrated to the Land of Israel. He is most famous for his *Or Hachayim*, a popular commentary on the Torah. The famed Jewish historian and bibliophile Rabbi Chaim Yosef David Azulai was among his most notable disciples.

Rabbi Chayim ibn Atar, Ohr Hachaim, Bereishit 18:1

הטעם שלא ביקרו ה' [עד היום השלישי] כדי שלא ידברו על מחלתו, כי בבוא מלך גדול מתעורר רעש בכל העולמות.

G-d did not visit Abraham until the third day so that they should not speak about his illness, for when the Great King arrives, there is much ado in all the worlds.

The Hardest Day

TEXT 13A

Rabbi Shmuel Eliezer Halevi Eidel's
(Maharsha)
1555–1632
Rabbi, author, and Talmudist. Rabbi Eidel's established a yeshivah in Posen, Poland, which was supported by his mother-in-law, Eidel (hence his surname is "Eidel's"). He is primarily known for his *Chidushei Halachot*, a commentary on the Talmud in which he resolves difficulties in the texts of the Talmud, Rashi, and *Tosafot*, and which is a basic work for those who seek an in-depth understanding of the Talmud; and for his *Chidushei Agadot*, his innovative commentary on the homiletic passages of the Talmud.

Rabbi Shmuel Eidel's, Chidushei Agadot Maharsha to Baba Metzia 86b

"ביום השלישי למילתו." ביום ג' החולשה גוברת יותר.

"On the third day from the circumcision." On the third day the weakness is most severe.

TEXT 13B

Rabbi Eliyahu Mizrachi, Commentary to Rashi on Bereishit 18:1

מסתבר שה' לא בא לשאול בשלומו אלא ביום היותר קשה למילה,
שהוא היום השלישי. כדכתיב 'ויהי ביום השלישי בהיותם כואבים'.

It is likely that G-d did not visit him until the most painful day after the circumcision, which is the third day. As it is written, "On the third day, when they [the people of Shechem] were in pain."

Rabbi Eliyahu Mizrachi
c. 1455 – 1525/26

Talmudist and posek, and an authority on Halachah. He is best known for his Sefer Mizrachi, a supercommentary on Rashi's commentary on the Torah. He is also known as Re'em (רא"ם), the Hebrew acronym for "Rabbi Eliyahu Mizrachi," coinciding with the Biblical name of an animal, sometimes translated as "unicorn." Born in Constantinople, Re'em was a distinguished Talmudist, and master of secular sciences. Mizrachi was eventually appointed as Chacham Bashi ("Grand Rabbi") of the Ottoman Empire; he held this position for the rest of his life.

Mitzvah=Connection

PARABLE

A large ship was approaching the port, where thousands of people waited to greet it. Amidst the crowd, a small boy eagerly waved his hand toward the ship. Those around him began to laugh. "Little boy, why are you waving your hand so eagerly?" The boy replied that he was waving to the ship's captain.

"Foolish child," they said. "Don't you know that your hand is so tiny? Why would the captain pay any attention to your wave?"

"Of course he will notice me," the boy replied, "You see, the captain is my father."

TEXT 14

Hayom Yom

In 1942, Rabbi Yosef Y. Schneersohn, the sixth rebbe of Chabad, gave his son-in-law, the future Rebbe, the task of compiling an anthology of Chasidic aphorisms and customs arranged according to the days of the year. In describing the completed product, Rabbi Yosef Yitzchak wrote that it is "a book that is small in format but bursting with pearls and diamonds of the choicest quality."

The Lubavitcher Rebbe, Hayom Yom, entry for 8 Cheshvan

מצווה לשון צוותא וחיבור והעושה מצווה מתחבר עם העצמות ברוך הוא, מצווה הציווי.

[T]he Hebrew word] "mitzvah" is etymologically related to [the Aramaic word] tzavta— "joining," or "attachment." Whoever performs a mitzvah becomes attached to the Essence of G-d, Who issues that particular command.

STORY

A poor man entered a synagogue during the morning prayers to collect charity. One of the Chasidim inside stuck his hand into his pocket and withdrew a coin to give the pauper. A few moments later, when the pauper had moved on, this individual went to find him, and gave him another coin. When this happened a third time, the poor man finally asked him, "I don't understand. Why didn't you just give me the entire amount the first time?"

The Chasid answered, "Each time I put my hand in my pocket, I need to overcome the inner voice telling me to keep the money for myself. I want to overcome that inclination as many times as possible. Because each time I do, I am experiencing the mitzvah of giving charity more deeply."

Third Temple: Made by G-d or by Man?

TEXT 15A

Shemot (Exodus) 15:17

תְּבִאֵמוֹ וְתִטָּעֵמוֹ בְּהַר נַחֲלָתְךָ מָכוֹן לְשִׁבְתְּךָ פָּעַלְתָּ ה' מִקְדָּשׁ אֲדֹנָי כּוֹנְנוּ יָדֶיךָ:

You shall bring them and plant them on the mount of Your heritage, directed toward Your habitation, which You made, O G-d; the sanctuary, O G-d, which Your hands founded.

TEXT 15B

Rashi, ad loc.

חביב בית המקדש, שהעולם נברא ביד אחת שנאמר אף ידי יסדה ארץ ומקדש בשתי ידיים.

The Temple is beloved, since, whereas the world was created with "one hand," as it is stated, "Even My hand [only **one** hand] laid the foundation of the earth," the Sanctuary will be built with "**two** hands."

Rabbi Shlomo Yitzchaki (Rashi)
1040–1105
Most noted biblical and Talmudic commentator. Born in Troyes, France, Rashi studied in the famed *yeshivot* of Mainz and Worms. His commentaries on the Pentateuch and the Talmud, which focus on the straightforward meaning of the text, appear in virtually every edition of the Talmud and Bible.

TEXT 16A

Maimonides, Mishneh Torah, Laws of Kings, 11:1

אם יעמוד מלך מבית דויד הוגה בתורה ועוסק במצות כדויד אביו כפי
תורה שבכתב ושבעל פה ויכוף כל ישראל לילך בה ולחזק בדקה וילחם
מלחמות ה' הרי זה בחזקת שהוא משיח אם עשה והצליח ובנה מקדש
במקומו וקבץ נדחי ישראל הרי זה משיח בודאי.

Rabbi Moshe ben Maimon (Maimonides, Rambam)
1135–1204

Halachist, philosopher, author, and physician. Maimonides was born in Cordoba, Spain. After the conquest of Cordoba by the Almohads, he fled Spain and eventually settled in Cairo, Egypt. There, he became the leader of the Jewish community and served as court physician to the vizier of Egypt. He is most noted for authoring the *Mishneh Torah*, an encyclopedic arrangement of Jewish law, and for his philosophical work, *Guide for the Perplexed*. His rulings on Jewish law are integral to the formation of halachic consensus.

If a king will arise from the House of David who diligently contemplates the Torah and observes its mitzvot as prescribed by the Written Law and the Oral Law as David, his ancestor; will compel all of Israel to walk in (the way of the Torah); rectify the breaches in its observance; fight the wars of G-d, we may, with assurance, **consider** him Moshiach.

If he succeeds in the above, and then builds the Temple in its place, and gathers the dispersed of Israel, he is **definitely** the Moshiach.

TEXT 16B

Maimonides, Pirush Hamishnayot, Introduction to Tractate Midot

והביא אחר תמיד מידות, ואין בו עניין אחר אלא סיפור, שהוא זוכר
מידת המקדש וצורתו ובניינו וכל עניינו. והתועלת שיש במין ההוא, כי
כשייבנה במהרה בימינו, יש לשמור ולעשות התבנית ההוא, והתבניות
והצורות והערך.

Tractate Midot *follows Tractate* Tamid *(which describes the sacrifices). Tractate* Midot *is purely narrative, recalling the dimensions of the Temple, its structure and form, and all other matters.*

The utility of this sort of narrative will be evident when the future Temple will be rebuilt. Then, we will seek to emulate the dimensions, structure, and image of the ancient Temple.

Putting on the Doors

TEXT 17A

The Lubavitcher Rebbe, Shaarei Geulah, vol. 2, p. 114

על הפסוק "טבעו בארץ שעריה", איתא במדרשי חז"ל, ששערי בית המקדש טבעו במקומם וכאשר ירד בית המקדש השלישי מן השמים, יעלו ויתגלו שערי בית המקדש ו[אנו] נעמידום במקומם.

The Midrash states that the gates of the Temple are buried in their place. When the Third Temple descends from Heaven, the gates will rise and be revealed. We will then set them in their place.

TEXT 17B

Ibid.

ולכאורה אינו מובן: מהו הצורך להשתמש בשערי בית המקדש שטבעו
באָרץ? הרי כשם שבית המקדש ירד מן השמים, יכולים לרדת גם שערי
המקדש מהשמים?

It is perplexing: Why is it necessary to use gates
that were buried underground? Just as the Temple
itself will descend from Heaven, can't the gates,
too, descend from Heaven?

TEXT 17C

Ibid.

מכיון שהקדוש ברוך הוא הוא תכלית הטוב וטבע הטוב להיטיב, בוודאי
רוצה למלא את רצונו של האדם 'שרוצה בקב שלו יותר מתשעה קבים
של חבירו', ולכן רוצה הקדוש ברוך הוא שגם בבית המקדש השלישי—
שירד מוכן מן השמים—יהיה גם העילוי דפעולת האדם, "קב שלו".

Because G-d is the ultimate goodness, and the
nature of goodness is to be kind, He most certainly wants to fulfill the desire of man. Man,
by nature, "prefers one measure of his own work than
nine measures of someone else's." Therefore, G-d wants
the Third Temple, which will descend from Heaven, to
also include our input, "one measure of our own work."

4

CHAYEI SARAH

Matchmaker, Make Me a Match

Dating in the Orthodox Jewish Community

PARASHA OVERVIEW
Chayei Sarah

Sarah dies at age 127 and is buried in the Machpelah Cave in Hebron, which Abraham purchases from Ephron the Hittite for four hundred shekels of silver.

Abraham's servant Eliezer is sent, laden with gifts, to Charan, to find a wife for Isaac. At the village well, Eliezer asks G-d for a sign: when the maidens come to the well, he will ask for some water to drink; the woman who will offer to give his camels to drink as well shall be the one destined for his master's son.

Rebecca, the daughter of Abraham's nephew Bethuel, appears at the well and passes the "test." Eliezer is invited to their home, where he repeats the story of the day's events. Rebecca returns with Eliezer to the land of Canaan, where they encounter Isaac praying in the field. Isaac marries Rebecca, loves her, and is comforted over the loss of his mother.

Abraham takes a new wife, Keturah (Hagar), and fathers six additional sons, but Isaac is designated as his only heir. Abraham dies at age 175 and is buried beside Sarah by his two eldest sons, Isaac and Ishmael.

Eliezer the Matchmaker

TEXT 1A

Bereishit (Genesis) 24:1–4

וְאַבְרָהָם זָקֵן בָּא בַּיָּמִים וַה' בֵּרַךְ אֶת אַבְרָהָם בַּכֹּל:

וַיֹּאמֶר אַבְרָהָם אֶל עַבְדּוֹ זְקַן בֵּיתוֹ הַמֹּשֵׁל בְּכָל אֲשֶׁר לוֹ שִׂים נָא יָדְךָ תַּחַת יְרֵכִי:

וְאַשְׁבִּיעֲךָ בַּה' אֱלֹקֵי הַשָּׁמַיִם וֵאלֹקֵי הָאָרֶץ אֲשֶׁר לֹא תִקַּח אִשָּׁה לִבְנִי מִבְּנוֹת הַכְּנַעֲנִי אֲשֶׁר אָנֹכִי יוֹשֵׁב בְּקִרְבּוֹ:

כִּי אֶל אַרְצִי וְאֶל מוֹלַדְתִּי תֵּלֵךְ וְלָקַחְתָּ אִשָּׁה לִבְנִי לְיִצְחָק:

Abraham was now old, advanced in years, and G-d had blessed Abraham in all things.

And Abraham said to the senior servant of his household, who was in charge of all that he owned, "Put your hand under my thigh.

"And I will make you swear by G-d, the G-d of heaven and the G-d of the earth, that you will not take a wife for my son from the daughters of the Canaanites among whom I dwell.

"But you will go to the land of my birth and get a wife for my son Isaac."

TEXT 1B

Ibid., 24:10–11

וַיִּקַּח הָעֶבֶד עֲשָׂרָה גְמַלִּים מִגְּמַלֵּי אֲדֹנָיו וַיֵּלֶךְ וְכָל טוּב אֲדֹנָיו בְּיָדוֹ וַיָּקָם
וַיֵּלֶךְ אֶל אֲרַם נַהֲרַיִם אֶל עִיר נָחוֹר:
וַיַּבְרֵךְ הַגְּמַלִּים מִחוּץ לָעִיר אֶל בְּאֵר הַמָּיִם לְעֵת עֶרֶב לְעֵת צֵאת הַשֹּׁאֲבֹת:

T hen the servant took ten of his master's camels
and set out, taking with him all the bounty of
his master; and he made his way to Aram-
Naharaim, to the city of Nahor.

*He made the camels kneel down by the well outside
the city, at evening time, the time when women come
out to draw water.*

TEXT 1C

Ibid., 24:22–27

וַיְהִי כַּאֲשֶׁר כִּלּוּ הַגְּמַלִּים לִשְׁתּוֹת וַיִּקַּח הָאִישׁ נֶזֶם זָהָב בֶּקַע מִשְׁקָלוֹ וּשְׁנֵי
צְמִידִים עַל יָדֶיהָ עֲשָׂרָה זָהָב מִשְׁקָלָם:
וַיֹּאמֶר בַּת מִי אַתְּ הַגִּידִי נָא לִי הֲיֵשׁ בֵּית אָבִיךְ מָקוֹם לָנוּ לָלִין:
וַתֹּאמֶר אֵלָיו בַּת בְּתוּאֵל אָנֹכִי בֶּן מִלְכָּה אֲשֶׁר יָלְדָה לְנָחוֹר:
וַתֹּאמֶר אֵלָיו גַּם תֶּבֶן גַּם מִסְפּוֹא רַב עִמָּנוּ גַּם מָקוֹם לָלוּן:
וַיִּקֹּד הָאִישׁ וַיִּשְׁתַּחוּ לַה':
וַיֹּאמֶר בָּרוּךְ ה' אֱלֹקֵי אֲדֹנִי אַבְרָהָם אֲשֶׁר לֹא עָזַב חַסְדּוֹ וַאֲמִתּוֹ מֵעִם אֲדֹנִי
אָנֹכִי בַּדֶּרֶךְ נָחַנִי ה' בֵּית אֲחֵי אֲדֹנִי:

When the camels had finished drinking, the man took a gold nose-ring weighing a half-shekel, and two gold bands for her arms, ten shekels in weight.

"Pray tell me," he said, "whose daughter are you? Is there room in your father's house for us to spend the night?"

She replied, "I am the daughter of Bethuel the son of Milcah, whom she bore to Nahor."

And she went on, "There is plenty of straw and feed at home, and also room to spend the night."

The man bowed low in homage to G-d.

And he said, "Blessed be G-d, the G-d of my master Abraham, who has not withheld His steadfast faithfulness from my master. For I have been guided on my errand by G-d, to the house of my master's kinsmen."

TEXT 1D

Ibid., 64–67

וַתִּשָּׂא רִבְקָה אֶת עֵינֶיהָ וַתֵּרֶא אֶת יִצְחָק וַתִּפֹּל מֵעַל הַגָּמָל:

וַתֹּאמֶר אֶל הָעֶבֶד מִי הָאִישׁ הַלָּזֶה הַהֹלֵךְ בַּשָּׂדֶה לִקְרָאתֵנוּ וַיֹּאמֶר הָעֶבֶד
הוּא אֲדֹנִי וַתִּקַּח הַצָּעִיף וַתִּתְכָּס:

וַיְסַפֵּר הָעֶבֶד לְיִצְחָק אֵת כָּל הַדְּבָרִים אֲשֶׁר עָשָׂה:

וַיְבִאֶהָ יִצְחָק הָאֹהֱלָה שָׂרָה אִמּוֹ וַיִּקַּח אֶת רִבְקָה וַתְּהִי לוֹ לְאִשָּׁה וַיֶּאֱהָבֶהָ
וַיִּנָּחֵם יִצְחָק אַחֲרֵי אִמּוֹ:

And Rebecca lifted her eyes and saw Isaac, and she let herself down from the camel. And she said to the servant, "Who is that man walking in the field towards us?" And the servant said, "He is my master." And she took the veil and covered herself.

The servant told Isaac all the things that he had done.

Isaac then brought her into the tent of his mother Sarah, and he took Rebeccah as his wife. Isaac loved her, and thus found comfort after his mother's death.

The Process

Proposal and Betrothal

TEXT 2

Maimonides, Mishneh Torah, Hilchot Ishut, 1:1

קודם מתן תורה היה אדם פוגע אשה בשוק אם רצה הוא והיא לישא
אותה מכניסה לתוך ביתו ובועלה בינו לבין עצמו ותהיה לו לאשה.
כיון שנתנה תורה נצטוו ישראל שאם ירצה האיש לישא אשה יקנה
אותה תחלה בפני עדים ואחר כך תהיה לו לאשה שנאמר "כי יקח איש
אשה ובא אליה."

Rabbi Moshe ben Maimon
(Maimonides, Rambam)
1135–1204

Halachist, philosopher, author, and physician. Maimonides was born in Cordoba, Spain. After the conquest of Cordoba by the Almohads, he fled Spain and eventually settled in Cairo, Egypt. There, he became the leader of the Jewish community and served as court physician to the vizier of Egypt. He is most noted for authoring the *Mishneh Torah*, an encyclopedic arrangement of Jewish law, and for his philosophical work, *Guide for the Perplexed*. His rulings on Jewish law are integral to the formation of halachic consensus.

Before the Torah was given, a man would meet a woman in the marketplace and if he and she desired to marry, he would bring her into his home, conduct relations in private, and she would be his wife.

Once the Torah was given, the Jews were commanded that when a man desires to marry a woman, he must first betroth her in the presence of witnesses. [Only] after this, does she become his wife. As [alluded to in] the verse [which] states, "When a man takes a wife and has relations with her..."

TEXT 2B

Ibid. 1:2–3

וליקוחין אלו מצות עשה של תורה הם. ובאחד משלשה דברים אלו
האשה נקנית: בכסף, או בשטר, או בביאה...

וליקוחין אלו הן הנקראין קידושין או אירוסין בכל מקום. ואשה שנקנית
באחד מג' דברים אלו היא הנקראת מקודשת או מאורסת.

וכיון שנקנית האשה ונעשית מקודשת אף על פי שלא נבעלה ולא
נכנסה לבית בעלה הרי היא אשת איש והבא עליה חוץ מבעלה חייב
מיתת בית דין ואם רצה לגרש צריכה גט.

This process of betrothal fulfills [one of] the Torah's positive commandments. The process of betrothing a wife is formalized in three ways: through [the transfer of] money, through [the transfer of a] betrothal document, and through marital relations…

This process is termed kidushin or eirusin *in all texts, and a woman who has been betrothed by way of one of these three means is described as* m'kudeshet *or* m'ureset.

Once this process of betrothal has been formalized and a woman has become mekudeshet, *she has the status of a married woman even though the marriage bond has not been consummated and she has not been brought into her husband's home. Should anyone other than her husband [to-be] engage in marital relations with her, he is liable for execution by the court. If he wishes to divorce her, she requires a get [halachic bill of divorce].*

TEXT 3

Ibid. 3:21

אף על פי שעיקר הדברים כן הוא נהגו כל ישראל לקדש בכסף או בשוה כסף, וכן אם רצה לקדש בשטר מקדש, אבל אין מקדשין בביאה לכתחלה ואם קידש בביאה מכין אותו מכת מרדות כדי שלא יהיו ישראל פרוצים בדבר זה אף על פי שקידושיו קידושין גמורין.

Although this is the letter of the law, all of Israel are accustomed to betroth through [the transfer of] money or an item of monetary value. If one wished to betroth by way of a document he may do so. However, one should not consecrate [a woman] through sexual relations. If a man consecrates [a woman] through sexual relations, he is given stripes for rebelliousness so that the Jewish people will not extend beyond the limits of modesty in this manner. Nevertheless, the kidushin are binding.

Consent

TEXT 4

Ibid. 4:1

אין האשה מתקדשת אלא לרצונה והמקדש אשה בעל כרחה
אינה מקודשת.

woman may only be betrothed voluntarily. If one forces a woman to be betrothed, she is not considered betrothed.

Nisu'in

TEXT 5

Ibid., 10:1-2

הארוסה אסורה לבעלה מדברי סופרים כל זמן שהיא בבית אביה. והבא
על ארוסתו בבית חמיו מכין אותו מכת מרדות. ואפילו אם קידשה
בביאה אסור לו לבוא עליה ביאה שנייה בבית אביה עד שיביא אותה
לתוך ביתו ויתיחד עמה ויפרישנה לו. וייחוד זה הוא הנקרא כניסה
לחופה וחוא הנקרא נישואין בכל מקום. והבא על ארוסתו לשם נישואין
אחר כיון שנכנסה הארוסה לחופה הרי זו מותרת לבא זליה בכל עת
שירצה והרי היא אשתו גמורה לכל דבר. ומשתכנס לחופה נקראת
נשואה אף על פי שלא נבעלה.

woman who has been betrothed (an arusah) is forbidden by Rabbinic law to engage in marital relations with her husband as long as she is living in her father's home. A man who has relations with his arusah in his father-in-law's home is punished with "stripes for rebelliousness" ... until he brings her into his home, is secluded with her, and dedicates her to him.

This seclusion is referred to as entry into the chuppah, and it is universally referred to as nisu'in [literally: marriage]....

Once an arusah has entered the chuppah, her husband is allowed to have relations with her at any time he desires, and she is considered to be his wife with regard to all matters. Once she enters the chuppah, she is called a nesu'ah, although [the couple] has not consummated the marriage.

The Two-in-One Marriage

TEXT 6

Rabbi Yakov Ben Asher
(Tur, Ba'al Haturim)
ca. 1269–1343
Halachic authority and codifier. Rabbi Ya'akov was born in Germany and moved to Toledo, Spain, with his father, the noted halachist Rabbeinu Asher, to escape persecution. He wrote *Arba'ah Turim*, an ingeniously organized and highly influential code of Jewish law. He is considered one of the greatest authorities of Halachah.

Rabbi Yakov ben Asher, Tur, Even Ha'Ezer, §62

והאידנא אין נוהגין ליארס אלא בשעת חופה, הלכך מברך ברכת אירוסין וברכת נישואין יחד זה אחר זה.

Nowadays, the custom is that eirusin is conducted only at the time of the chuppah. Therefore, the blessings for eirusin and nisu'in are recited together, one after another.

Down the Timeline

Pre-Preliminary (a.k.a. "Engagement")

TEXT 7A

Talmud Tractate Kiddushin, 12b

דרב מנגיד על דמקדש בשוקא ועל דמקדש בביאה ועל דמקדש בלא שידוכי.

Rav would give lashes to one who betrothed a woman in the street, to one who consecrated through intercourse, and to one who consecrated without shidduchin.

Babylonian Talmud
A literary work of monumental proportions that draws upon the legal, spiritual, intellectual, ethical, and historical traditions of Judaism. The 37 tractates of the Babylonian Talmud contain the teachings of the Jewish sages from the period after the destruction of the 2nd Temple through the 5th century CE. It has served as the primary vehicle for the transmission of the Oral Law and the education of Jews over the centuries; it is the entry point for all subsequent legal, ethical, and theological Jewish scholarship.

TEXT 7B

Ibid., 41a

דאמר רב יהודה אמר רב אסור לאדם שיקדש את האשה עד שיראנה שמא יראה בה דבר מגונה ותתגנה עליו ורחמנא אמר "ואהבת לרעך כמוך."

For Rabbi Yehuda said in the name of Rav: It is prohibited for a man to betroth (mekadesh) a woman until he has seen her. For [if he does not, then once he does betroth her,] perhaps he will find something unappealing about her, and he will be repulsed by her. [Thus he will have violated that which] the Torah says, "And you shall love your fellow as yourself."

TEXT 8

Rabbi Shlomo Yitzchaki
(Rashi)
1040–1105
Most noted biblical and Talmudic commentator. Born in Troyes, France, Rashi studied in the famed *yeshivot* of Mainz and Worms. His commentaries on the Pentateuch and the Talmud, which focus on the straightforward meaning of the text, appear in virtually every edition of the Talmud and Bible.

Rashi to Tractate Pesachim 49a, s.v. Seudah shniah

כך הוא דרך התתנים לאחר סעודת אירוסין חוזר ומשגר סבלונות לארוסתו וסועד שם.

*S*uch is the custom of grooms: After the betrothal (eirusin) feast, he again sends gifts to his betrothed, and feasts there.

TEXT 9

Rabbi Yom Tov Asevilli, Responsa of the Ritva, ch. 68

מנהג כל בני עירכם לעשות שידוכין בלא קידושין ולתת סבלונות בשעת שידוכין או אחרי שידוכין ואחרי כן מקדשין סמוך לחופה, ואין אחד שיקדש ואחר כך יתן מתנות.

Rabbi Yomtov Asevilli
(Ritva)
ca. 1250–1330
Spanish rabbi and Talmudist. Ritva was born in Seville. He is mostly known for his Talmudic commentary, which is extremely clear, and to this day, remains most frequently quoted and used.

*I*t is the custom of all the people of your city to perform the engagement (shidduchin) without betrothal (kiddushin), and to give gifts at the time of the engagement, or afterwards. Only then does the betrothal take place, in proximity to the chuppah; there is no one who first betroths, and then gives gifts.

Pre-Pre-Preliminary (a.k.a. "Courtship")

TEXT 10

Rabbi Nissim ben Reuven of Gerona, Commentary on Rif, Shabbos 5b, s.v. Ein meshadchin

"אין משדכין". מלשון שקט ומנוחה שהאשה מוצאת בבית בעלה כדכתיב "ומצאן מנוחה אשה בית אישה," ומתרגמינן "ותשקוט הארץ—ושדוכת ארעא".

It is derived from the quietude and comfort that a woman finds in her husband's house, as it is written, "May you find rest, each woman in her husband's house." The Aramaic translation for "and the land rested" is ve'shiduchat ara'a.

Rabbi Nisim ben Reuven "the Ran" of Gerona
1320–1380
Influential talmudist and authority on Jewish law; among the last great Spanish talmudic scholars. Considered the outstanding halachic authority of his generation, queries came to him from throughout the Diaspora. His works include commentaries on the Talmud and on Rabbi Yitzchak Alfasi's code, responsa literature, a commentary on the Bible, and a collection of sermons, *Derashot Haran*, which elucidates fundamentals of Judaism.

The Matchmaker

TEXT 11

Rabbi Moshe Isserles, Glosses of the Rema to Choshen Mishpat, 185:10

השדכן הוי כמו סרסור ואם השדכן רוצה שישלמו לו מיד שכר שדכנותו
והבעלים אינם רוצים לשלם עד הנשואין תלוי במנהג המדינה ובמקום
שאין מנהג הדין עם הבעלים.

Rabbi Moshe Isserles
(Rema)
1525–1572

Halachist. Rama served as rabbi in Krakow, Poland, and is considered the definitive authority on Jewish law among Ashkenazic Jewry. Rema authored glosses on the Shulchan Aruch (known as the *Mapah*) and *Darchei Moshe*, a commentary on the halachic compendium *Arba'ah Turim*.

A matchmaker is like a middleman. If the matchmaker wants to be paid immediately [upon making the match] for his service in making the match, and the [families of the engaged couple] do not wish to pay before the marriage, [the law] depends on local custom. In the absence of prevailing custom, the law accords with the [families].

"It's a Shidduch!"

Arranged Marriages

TEXT 12

Shulchan Aruch Yoreh Dei'ah, 240:25

תלמיד שרוצה ללכת למקום אחר, שהוא בוטח שיראה סימן ברכה
בתלמודו לפני הרב ששם, ואביו מוחה בו... אינו צריך לשמוע לאביו בזה.
הגה: וכן אם האב מוחה בבן לישא איזו אשה שיחפוץ בה הבן, אין צריך
לשמוע אל האב.

A student who wishes to go to a particular place [of Torah study] where he is confident that he will see success in his studies with the teacher there, and his father protests ... he does not need to listen to his father in this matter.

Gloss: So, too, if a father protests against his son marrying a woman of his choosing, he does not need to listen to his father.

A Divine Institution

TEXT 13

Rabbi Menachem Mendel Schneerson
1902–1994

The towering Jewish leader of the 20th century, known as "the Lubavitcher Rebbe," or simply as "the Rebbe." Born in southern Ukraine, the Rebbe escaped Nazi-occupied Europe, arriving in the U.S. in June 1941. The Rebbe inspired and guided the revival of traditional Judaism after the European devastation, impacting virtually every Jewish community the world over. The Rebbe often emphasized that the performance of just one additional good deed could usher in the era of Moshiach. The Rebbe's scholarly talks and writings have been printed in more than 200 volumes.

The Lubavitcher Rebbe, Igrot Kodesh, vol. 14, p. 345

שבכלל כל ענין שידוך וזיווג הוא למעלה מדרך הטבע וכמאמר רז"ל
הידוע המדמה זה לקריאת ים סוף, וכמו שכתוב "ומה' אשה משכלת".

The entire matter of a shidduch and marriage transcends the bounds of nature, as per the well-known statement of our Sages who likened marriage to the splitting of the sea.

STORY

The story is told that a Roman matron once asked Rabbi Yose: "How has your G-d been occupying His time since He finished the creation of the world?" "He has been busy pairing couples," answered the rabbi.

She was astonished. "Is that His trade? Even I can do that job. As many man-servants and maid-servants as I have, I can pair."

"Perhaps it is a simple matter in your eyes," replied the rabbi. "For G-d, it is as intricate as the splitting of the sea."

She promptly placed one thousand man-servants opposite one thousand maid-servants and declared, "He will marry her, she will marry him," and so on.

The next morning, two thousand servants came to her door, beaten and bruised, complaining, "I do not want her, I do not want him!"

She sent for Rabbi Yose, and conceded: "Rabbi, your Torah is true." The Talmud explains: Matchmaking was a simple matter in her eyes because she, unlike G-d, could not

---

understand the fundamental differences in the human character that factor into one stranger being successfully matched with another.

There is no doubt, the Talmudic Sages conclude, that G-d Himself had to be the first and ultimate *shadchan* (matchmaker). Who else could blend two disparate personalities so that they cleave together "as one flesh"? Did he not arrange the union of Adam and Eve? The conclusion was irresistible, and it was written no fewer than five times in midrashic literature: "Marriages are made in Heaven."

This is not a romantic American cliché, but a serious statement of predestination. G-d determines which people will unite successfully and serve as vehicles for human survival.

Does not the Talmud say: "Forty days before the birth of a child, a heavenly voice proclaims: 'The daughter of so-and-so will be married to so-and-so'"? The Talmud even illustrates how this idea induced a spirit of resignation in some people, with the tale of a young woman who refused to wear pretty clothes, jewelry, or cosmetics to attract a husband, because she believed that—regardless of what she might do—her suitor would be brought to her by G-d.

STORY

The saintly Rabbi Yisroel of Ruzhin had an unusual custom when it came to matchmaking. He would give a sizable monetary gift to anyone who suggested a match for one of his children, even if the couple didn't hit it off and the match didn't work out. It is customary to pay a matchmaker when a successful match is made. But to pay a matchmaker for a mismatch was unheard of. So why did Rabbi Yisroel do just that? He explained:

In heaven it is announced who your soul mate is before you are born. An angel looks at your soul and then calls out the name of your soul mate. But do you think the angel gets it right the first time? Not always. Often the angel suggests a name, and G-d nixes it. So the angel proposes another possible soul mate, and again G-d says no. Sometimes a long list of names is called out until the right one is reached and G-d gives His approval. Each one of those names has the potential to be your soul mate. But only one is destined to be yours.

Then your soul comes down here to this world and starts its search for the one. What you don't realize is that you need to meet all those other potential soul mates before you can meet your ultimate one. That's why I pay not only a matchmaker who is successful, but even one who suggests a match that doesn't work out.

Because every failed relationship brings you one step closer to your soul mate.

This gives a whole new perspective on dates that go nowhere and relationships that fizzle out. They should not leave us jaded or discouraged. The lessons we learn and the experiences we gain are necessary rungs on our ladder to happiness.

So, should you go on every blind date anyone ever suggests? Should you indiscriminately meet any random person, just to tally up the necessary bad dates and get to the real thing? Rabbi Yisroel answered that one too.

There was once a sly character in his community who was short on cash. He thought he could make a quick buck by suggesting a random match for one of Rabbi Yisroel's sons. Knowing he would be paid even if it failed, he mentioned the name of the first single girl that came to mind. Rabbi Yisroel heard his suggestion patiently and said, "Some matches seem good to angels in heaven. Others at least seem reasonable to people on earth. Yours is neither."

The Pull of the Heart

TEXT 14A

Rabbi Yosef Yitzchak of Lubavitch,
Igrot Kodesh, Rebbe Rayatz, vol. 12, p. 113

בטח זוכר הוא מה שאמרתי לו שאחר שידוך טוב צריכים לחזור ושלא
לקמץ בזמן נסיעות לחזיון.

Surely you remember what I told you—that one must actively seek out a good shidduch. One should not be miserly with regard to the times invested in traveling to see [a prospective partner].

Rabbi Yosef Yitzchak Schneersohn
(Rayats, Frierdiker Rebbe, Previous Rebbe)
1880–1950

Chasidic rebbe, prolific writer, and Jewish activist. Rabbi Yosef Yitzchak, the 6th leader of the Chabad movement, actively promoted Jewish religious practice in Soviet Russia and was arrested for these activities. After his release from prison and exile, he settled in Warsaw, Poland, from where he fled Nazi occupation, and arrived in New York in 1940. Settling in Brooklyn, Rabbi Schneersohn worked to revitalize American Jewish life. His son-in law, Rabbi Menachem Mendel Schneerson, succeeded him as the leader of the Chabad movement.

STORY

In my late teens, I found myself in a quandary. I was preparing to graduate from high school, and I was unsure what to do next. I felt torn between my desire to further my Jewish education and my wish to pursue academic studies and embark upon a career.

Reading through *The Lubavitcher Rebbe's Memoirs*, written by the sixth Lubavitcher Rebbe, Rabbi Yosef Yitzchak Schneersonh, of righteous memory, the lyrical descriptions of vibrant early Chasidic history captivated me. I loved the images of deep Torah study combined with a close bond with nature that the book portrayed, and I began to feel a deep connection to Chabad.

Thus, faced with the dilemma of my immediate future, I wrote my first letter to the Lubavitcher Rebbe, Rabbi Menachem Mendel Schneerson, of righteous memory.

The Rebbe's response arrived quickly. Its content surprised me, and I realized that I had expected the Rebbe to simply say, "Don't go to college." In fact, the Rebbe advised me to defer my college education for a year or two until I had a more solid background in Torah learning and Jewish values. This would also provide a stronger yardstick with which to evaluate my academic studies.

I followed the Rebbe's advice, and, at the age of eighteen, began attending Beth Jacob Teachers' Seminary in Williamsburg. At the time it was the most highly regarded institution of advanced Jewish education for young women.

Each day, after school, I went to work as a part-time nanny in the house of a prominent rabbinic educator. While tending to the children, I unknowingly drew the attention of an older couple who lived nearby. The couple approached me and explained that they had noticed my love for Torah, and wanted to pay my way to Israel to meet a young man who headed a kabbalistic seminary. They were convinced we would be a good match for marriage.

At the time, I had no one to ask for advice about such a serious matter. The offer sounded exotic and interesting, but I wasn't sure it was right for me. The well-meaning couple really didn't know me nor did they know what I was looking for in a life-partner. How could they suggest a soul mate for me?

Feeling very alone, I had a strong yearning to travel to the Crown Heights neighborhood of Brooklyn, New York, where Chabad-Lubavitch headquarters were located.

By the time I arrived at 770 Eastern Parkway, I felt so emotionally overwhelmed that I sat outside the building sobbing.

An elderly gentleman with a wispy beard approached me and asked me what was wrong. I explained that I had written a few letters to the Rebbe in my earlier teens and now I wished to speak with him.

"Wait here a minute," murmured the gentleman, and he went inside the stately brick building. I later found out that he was the Rebbe's senior secretary, Rabbi Hodakov.

Rabbi Hodakov returned a while later and informed me I had an appointment with the Rebbe the very next day. Little did I know that I was not following the protocol for arranging a meeting, or that one usually needed to make an appointment months in advance.

The next day, after a sleepless night, I took my turn to enter the Rebbe's study. My knees felt like jelly, and I held onto the desk for support. But as soon as I looked into the Rebbe's calm, clear, compassionate blue eyes, I was able to relax slightly.

I explained my situation as concisely as I could, and the Rebbe responded briefly, directly addressing my concern. "He (the prospective groom) is there [in Israel] and you are here. You are very different from each other."

Then he added, speaking in Yiddish (though I have no idea how the Rebbe knew that I understood the language), "Remove him from your agenda."

I walked out exhilarated and relieved, not just because I had received a direct answer from someone I trusted, but because I no longer felt alone in the world. I had found a guide, a mentor.

A short time later, someone else suggested a young businessman as a suitable match for me. I met with him a few times, but I was unsure if he was truly my soul mate.

This time, I went into the office of the Rebbe's secretariat and asked to make an appointment with the Rebbe.

My appointment was set for a week later, once again, highly unusual considering the typical wait for a meeting.

This time, the Rebbe took the initiative in asking me questions, "Do you like this man?"

It was an obvious question, but to me, coming from a rabbi, a totally unexpected one. I gulped before replying, "I have stam *ahavat Yisrael* [basic love of a fellow Jew] for him."

The Rebbe grinned from ear to ear with the confidential smile of a close relative.

He responded, again in Yiddish, *"Far a man darf men hoben mer vi stam ahavas Yisroel* [For a husband, one must have more than plain, basic love of a fellow Jew."

TEXT 14B

The Lubavitcher Rebbe, Igrot Kodesh, vol. 6, p. 338

ברכה ושלום!

במענה על מכתבה מג' אלול, נעם לי לקרא במכתבה מה שכותבת שהכירה כמה מעלות בהאישיות שלו ומתאים למה שרוצה למצוא בבחור שתנשא לו, וגם מקוה שאולי ישנם בו עוד מעלות שעדיין לא נגלו לפני'.

נכון הוא מה שכותבת שבענין כזה צריך להיות קיים גם רגש חיובי מסויים ולא רק חשבון על פי השכל, ומובן הוא גם כן שהרי בונים בית שלם בנין עדי עד, שצריך להיות הבית אחיד בכל העניניים ולא רק בעניני שכל, אבל לאידך גיסא, לא בכל פעם בנקל לברר איפוא מסתיים שקול הדבר הבא מצד השכל ומתחיל שקול הדבר הבא מצד הרגש, כי לפעמים רבות, אף שנדמה שאין זה אלא ענין שבשכל, הרי באמת יש כאן חלק גדול ואולי גם חלק המכריע של הרגש, ותקותי אשר אחר שתפגש אתו עוד פעמים תוכל לברר זה בעצמה, שלא רק שכל בדבר אלא גם רגש.

בהתאם להנ"ל הנה אם ברור הדבר שלעת עתה אין כל רגש בדבר, הרי כנראה שעוד מוקדמת ההחלטה בזה, אבל אם גם הרגש משתתף בזה, הרי יהי רצון מה' יתברך שיהיה בהצלחה ובשעה טובה ומוצלחת.

I was pleased to read in your letter that you found many positive qualities in his [the young man you have been meeting's] personality, and that he fits the bill with regard to what you are looking for in a young man whom you wish to marry. You also hope that maybe there are additional [fine] qualities that have as yet not become known to you.

You are correct when you write that in matters such as these, there must be some positive emotional feelings [toward the young man] as well, not only that it makes sense intellectually.

This is logically understandable as well: Marriage consists of constructing a complete edifice, one that will endure for all eternity. As such, it must be an edifice and home that is united and coupled in all aspects [in emotional aspects as well], not only joined intellectually.

On the other hand, one cannot always easily discern where the intellectual deliberations end and the emotional considerations begin. Quite often, although one may think that [his or her position on the matter] is purely a matter of intellectual reflection, in point of fact, it is in large part—if not overwhelmingly so—a matter of emotional consideration.

It is therefore my hope that after you meet with him additional times you will be able to discern this matter for yourself—that there is not only intellect in the matter [of your appreciation for him], but emotion as well.

In light of the above, if you are sure that as of yet you harbor no emotional feelings at all then it would seem that it is too soon to make a decision regarding this matter. However, if you see that [positive] emotional feelings are also integrated [in your appreciation for him], then may it be G-d's will that the shidduch be with success and in a good and auspicious hour.

Not a Romance Novel

STORY

It happened a long time ago. I remember exactly when it happened because it was the year of our great tragedy. We had been in the United States for only five years, having arrived from Stockholm, Sweden, where my father, Rabbi Yacov Yisroel Zuber, of blessed memory, had been sent as a Lubavitch emissary for nearly two decades.

The adjustment had been very difficult, but at this stage everything was falling into place. My father was the dean of the Lubavitcher School in Boston. He was an important member of the rabbinical court of the city, and had progressed from rabbi at a smaller synagogue in Dorchester to a larger congregation in Roxbury. My mother, Rebetzin Zlata Zuber, of blessed memory, was taking English classes at night, participating in women's auxiliaries and organizations and socializing in the new community.

And then, the tragedy struck.

One day I was an innocent, carefree student; the next, a devastated, bewildered, young adult. There was an abrupt change from childhood into the ugly, gruesome world of adult reality.

In today's world where crime and violence have become a part of everyday life, we might react with less intensity to brutal acts, but in 1953 the world was safer and more stable, so the news of our great loss was publicized not only locally and nationally, but all over the world.

Early one winter evening, just as the secular new year began, my father lost his life at the hands of unknown assailants, and our lives were forever changed.

And this is where my story actually begins. A few months

later, my mother decided we should go to New York for a private audience with the Rebbe, Rabbi Menachem Mendel Schneerson, of righteous memory.

I had been in an audience with the sixth Chabad Rebbe, Rabbi Yosef Yitzchak Schneersohn, of righteous memory, twice. Once, when I was a very young child, we visited him at the Grand Hotel in Stockholm when he was on his way to America. Immediately upon our arrival in the United States was the second time. But this time it would be very different. Rabbi Yosef Yitzchak, now known as the Previous Rebbe, had passed away about three years earlier, and we were going to have an audience with the new Rebbe of Lubavitch, Rabbi Menachem Mendel.

My memories of the Previous Rebbe were very clear—a dignified, large man, somber—a very serious looking person. I felt overawed and somewhat intimidated by him. But now things were different. My life had changed—I was no longer a child within a family, but a responsible, young adult. I thought the audience would be an interesting experience, and of course I wanted to carry out my mother's wishes to accompany her, but I had no idea what to expect.

Appointments for the audience were made weeks in advance; the names were written down and time slots assigned. The times were arbitrary, however, because it was quite impossible to know the exact length of time of each audience before us. There were often last-minute changes for dignitaries, visitors from far-away places, and emergencies. We were told to keep in touch with one of the Rebbe's aides, Rabbi Leibel Groner, during the specified evening so that we would not have to stand in the lobby for any great length of time.

There was a hushed silence inside 770, as Lubavitch World Headquarters became known, when we arrived. Some people waited right outside the office of the Rebbe, some in the outer hall. It wasn't very crowded. The audiences began in the evening, and often continued until the early hours of the morning.

Rabbi Groner kept track of the time and would knock on the door to the Rebbe's office, or even open the door, to signal that time was up. If the Rebbe was engrossed in conversation, he would disregard the interruption. From the list that Rabbi Groner had, we knew when it would be our turn.

My mother was visibly distressed. She was now the head of our family, a position for which she was quite unprepared. She was overwhelmed by the loss, the strange language, and the newness of the country.

Tension built up as we waited. The silence became stifling. And finally it was our turn. We were quickly ushered into the room. The Rebbe was sitting behind a large mahogany desk, facing the door. Two empty chairs were facing the Rebbe's desk, but we stood behind the chairs as is the custom. Around the room were bookcases filled with books of Jewish learning and I think there were piles of scholarly books near the bookcases as well.

My mother was crying softly while I glanced at the Rebbe. He looked at us with great compassion and concern: he had known my father well, and had been involved with us in the aftermath of the tragedy. Then he smiled gently and invited us to sit down. He seemed so human, so warm, I immediately felt at ease. He spoke to my mother for a length of time—of her plans for the future, about her daily activities, about my father, and everything of concern to our life.

Then the Rebbe turned to me and asked about my courses, my future plans, and my interest and concerns. It was without difficulty that I responded. He seemed so genuinely interested in everything I said, and from his responses and interjections, I knew he was listening carefully to everything. The bell rang, time was up, and we walked out feeling comforted and reassured.

I clearly remember my mother remarking that she was surprised at my interaction with the Rebbe, that I seemed so comfortable and at ease, as if he were a family member, someone I had known all my life. And indeed that is how I felt.

A few months later, when I went on a visit to New York with some friends, I decided to go see the Rebbe again. The appointment was made from Boston, and on the specified date I arrived at 770. I felt somewhat awkward waiting alone. I didn't know many people in the area, and no one in the lobby area that night. And then my turn came, and I was very excited to have the opportunity to meet with the Rebbe again. Now that I knew what to expect, my enthusiasm was quite boundless.

At first we discussed my studies. The Rebbe asked at length about my courses, my professors, and my interests and plans for the future. Then, to my great surprise, he asked me about my very personal plans, about my dating to get married. I told him that I had met several young men, but I had not met someone I wanted to marry.

The Rebbe smiled broadly and asked my opinion about a specific student.

I swallowed hard; I could not believe it, but the question concerned a young man I had recently met.

The Rebbe then asked about another student, and a third, and I was totally overwhelmed.

He apparently knew everything about my life, certainly in this aspect. I just shook my head and blushingly explained why each one was not the right one for me.

Then the Rebbe chuckled lightly and told me that I read too many books. How did he know? But know he did. Love, he explained to me, is not that which is portrayed in romantic novels. It isn't that overwhelming, blinding emotion that is portrayed in a romance. These books do not portray real life, he said. It is a fantasy world, a make-believe.

world with made-up emotions. Fiction is just that—fiction—but real life is different.

And then, as a father to a daughter, he began to explain to me the meaning of real love.

Love, he told me, is an emotion that increases in strength throughout life. It is sharing and caring and respecting one another. It is building a life together, a unit of family and home. The love that you feel as a young bride, he continued, is only the beginning of real love. It is through the small, everyday acts of living together that love flourishes and grows.

And so, he continued, the love you feel after five years or ten years is a gradual strengthening of bonds. As two lives unite to form one, with time, one reaches a point where each partner feels a part of the other, where each partner no longer can visualize life without his mate by his side.

Smilingly he told me to put aside the romantic notions developed by my literary involvement, and view love and marriage in a meaningful way.

I walked out of the Rebbe's office with a huge smile on my face. The Rebbe knew how to communicate with a dreamy young girl. He knew what to say and how to say it. His words, spoken from the heart, reverberated within my heart. That is my Rebbe.

From all over the world rabbis, businessmen, community leaders, and politicians sought the advice of the Rebbe, frequently on issues of far-reaching significance, affecting large numbers of people. Yet, in the case of a young girl standing at the threshold to life, preparing to make the most crucial decision of her life, to this young maiden he gave his undivided attention. With fatherly love and compassion, with patience and concern, he presented her with a life-long understanding of the meaning of love, marriage, home, and family.

STORY

There was a young woman who was supposed to marry a young man. They had never met, as it was an arranged marriage. So, the day approached, and the young man came to the home of the young woman to meet with her before the wedding. To the bride's astonishment she saw that her fiancé had a profoundly hunched back. She told her father to cancel the wedding; she could not marry this man. The father broke the news gently to the young man. He accepted the news graciously, but he asked if he could meet with her just one more time. She agreed.

They met again, and he told her the story of his hunched back. "When our soul was separated into two halves in Heaven, G-d decreed that you would have this hunched back, so I begged and pleaded that He would give it to me instead, that I would carry this burden, and not you." The young woman heard the truth in his words and with a whole and grateful heart, agreed to marry him.

It's Not All About Dollars and Cents

TEXT 14C

Ibid., vol. 6, p. 61

שלום וברכה,

איך האב ערהאלטען אייער בריף פון 5/13 אין וועלכען איר פרעגט אין נאמען פון אייער זון, א עצה וועגען דעם שידוך וואס מען לייגט אים פאר, און בא עם איז ניט זיכער אויב די עלטערן פון דער מיידעל וועלען עם קאנען ארויסהעלפען מיט גרעסערע סומעס.

מיין מיינונג אין דער איז, וויבאלד אז איר שרייבט אז זי האט מעלות
וועלכע פאסען פאר אייער זון, דאס איז דער עיקר בא א שידוך, און
וועגען פרנסה וועט זיי השי"ת העלפען, און מן הסתם וועלען אויף
דער ערשטער צייט לכל הפחות די עלטערען פון ביידע צדדים
ארויסהעלפען, און בפרט אז איר שרייבט אז די עלטערן פון דער
מיידעל האבען א פאבריק.

I received your letter of May 13th in which you ask—in your son's name—my advice regarding the shidduch that is being suggested for him. Your son is not sure if the parents of the girl will be able to assist [the young couple] with large sums of money.

My opinion is, that since you write that she has qualities that are suitable for your son, this is what is most important regarding a shidduch.

With regard to livelihood, G-d will help them. Most probably, at least at the beginning of their marriage, the parents of both parties will assist them. Especially considering that which you write, that the girl's parents own a factory.

Ignoring Insignificant Ethnic Markers

TEXT 14D

Ibid., vol. 19, p. 391

It is self-evident and patently simple that there is absolutely no room for anxiety and setting up a boundary, G-d forbid, between Ashkenazim and Sefardim. Especially so when in most recent years [we have witnessed] so many [Ashkenazim and Sefardim] who have become engaged to each other, and they have established their homes on the foundations of Torah and mitzvot, living fortunate and happy lives both materially as well as spiritually.

5

Truth or Consequences

Is It Ever Okay to Lie?

Dedicated in honor of the wedding of Menachem Klein and Mussie Sasonkin, 6 Kislev 5777.
May they build an everlasting edifice, and be a continuous source of nachas and joy to their families and Klal Yisroel.

PARASHA OVERVIEW
Toldot

Isaac and Rebecca endure twenty childless years, until their prayers are answered and Rebecca conceives. She experiences a difficult pregnancy as the "children struggle inside her"; G-d tells her that "there are two nations in your womb," and that the younger will prevail over the elder.

Esau emerges first; Jacob is born clutching Esau's heel. Esau grows up to be "a cunning hunter, a man of the field"; Jacob is "a wholesome man," a dweller in the tents of learning. Isaac favors Esau; Rebecca loves Jacob. Returning exhausted and hungry from the hunt one day, Esau sells his birthright (his rights as the firstborn) to Jacob for a pot of red lentil stew.

In Gerar, in the land of the Philistines, Isaac presents Rebecca as his sister, out of fear that he will be killed by someone coveting her beauty. He farms the land, reopens the wells dug by his father Abraham, and digs a series of his own wells: over the first two there is strife with the Philistines, but the waters of the third well are enjoyed in tranquility.

Esau marries two Hittite women. Isaac grows old and blind, and expresses his desire to bless Esau before he dies. While Esau goes off to hunt for his father's favorite food, Rebecca dresses Jacob in Esau's clothes, covers his arms and neck with goatskins to simulate the feel of his hairier brother, prepares a similar dish, and sends Jacob to his father. Jacob receives his father's blessings for "the dew of the heaven and the fat of the land" and mastery over his brother. When Esau returns and the deception is revealed, all Isaac can do for his weeping son is to predict that he will live by his sword, and that when Jacob falters, the younger brother will forfeit his supremacy over the elder.

Jacob leaves home for Charan to flee Esau's wrath and to find a wife in the family of his mother's brother, Laban. Esau marries a third wife—Machalath, the daughter of Ishmael.

Introduction

TEXT 1

Rabbi Ovadiah Yosef
1920–2013
Born in Basra, Iraq; talmudic scholar and former Sephardic chief rabbi of Israel. Rabbi Yosef is recognized as a modern authority in Halachah. His responsa are highly regarded within rabbinic circles and are considered binding in many Sephardic communities. He has also become a major political figure in Israel, serving as the spiritual leader of the Shas party. Among his most popular works are *Yabi'a Omer* and *Yechaveh Da'at*.

Rabbi Ovadiah Yosef, Sha'alot U'Teshuvot Yabia Omer,
vol. 8, Yoreh Dei'ah, ch. 32

נשאלתי אודות אישה שבהיותה צעירה פנויה, חייתה חיי אישות עם
בחור אחד ונתעברה ממנו וכשהוכר עוברה הלכה אצל רופא ועשה לה
הפלה מלאכותית. אחר כך עברה משם לעיר אחרת וחזרה בתשובה
שלמה בשמירת תורת ומצוות ונישאה לבחור ישיבה החרד לדבר ה'
וחיו יחדיו באהבה ואחווה ונתעברה ממנו וילדה לו בן זכר, והנה הביע
רצונו לקיים מצות פדיון הבן כהלכת גוברין יהודאין כי לא ידע שקודם
נישואיו עם אשתו, נתעברה כבר מאיש אחר והפילה כשהוכר עוברה.
והאישה באה אל הרב המקומי וסיפרה לו כל מה שאירע לה ושואל
הרב, האם חייב הוא להודיע לבעלה כדי להצילו מעוון ברכה לבטלה של
פדיון הבן, למרות שאם יודיע לו כל הקורות לאשתו קודם נישואיו, יופר
שלום הבית ועלול הדבר קרוב לוודאי שתפרוץ ביניהם מריבה וקטטה
ואחריתה מי ישורנו שאולי יבואו גם לידי גירושין, או שמא יש לומר
גדול השלום, שאפילו שם שמים שנכתב בקדושה נמחק מפני השלום,
ולכן שב ואל תעשה עדיף?

A young, single lady had an abortion upon finding out that she was pregnant. After some time, she changed her lifestyle, became religious, settled down, and married a yeshivah student.

When the happy day came and the couple was blessed with a baby boy, she now faced a serious dilemma. Her husband was planning on performing the Pidyon Haben (redemption of the firstborn) ceremony. This ceremony can only be performed if the newborn male is the firstborn child of the mother, excluding a case in which an abortion had been previously performed. Now, a central part of the ceremony is the recital of certain blessings that mention G-d's name, permissible only when it is indeed a legitimate case of Pidyon Ha-ben. However, in this case, inasmuch as the child was not the real firstborn, reciting the blessings would, in fact, be a grave sin of mentioning G-d's name in vain.

The lady confided to her local rabbi, asking what she should do. Is she obligated to tell her husband of her previous abortion and prevent him from saying G-d's name in vain, all the while running the risk of ruining domestic harmony, possibly leading to strife or divorce, G-d forbid? Or, perhaps she should remain silent and allow her husband to perform the ceremony in his innocence, thus eliminating the likely chance of domestic discord?

Truth Changing in the Bible

TEXT 2A

Bereishit (Genesis) 12:11–13

וַיְהִי כַּאֲשֶׁר הִקְרִיב לָבוֹא מִצְרָיְמָה וַיֹּאמֶר אֶל שָׂרַי אִשְׁתּוֹ הִנֵּה נָא יָדַעְתִּי כִּי אִשָּׁה יְפַת מַרְאֶה אָתְּ:

וְהָיָה כִּי יִרְאוּ אֹתָךְ הַמִּצְרִים וְאָמְרוּ אִשְׁתּוֹ זֹאת וְהָרְגוּ אֹתִי וְאֹתָךְ יְחַיּוּ:

אִמְרִי נָא אֲחֹתִי אָתְּ לְמַעַן יִיטַב לִי בַעֲבוּרֵךְ וְחָיְתָה נַפְשִׁי בִּגְלָלֵךְ:

Now, it came to pass when he drew near to come to Egypt, that Abram said to Sarai his wife, "Behold, now I know that you are a woman of fair appearance."

"And it will come to pass when the Egyptians see you, that they will say, 'This is his wife,' and they will slay me and let you live.

"Please say [that] you are my sister, in order that it go well with me because of you, and that my soul may live because of you."

TEXT 2B

Ibid., 26:6–7

וַיֵּשֶׁב יִצְחָק בִּגְרָר:

וַיִּשְׁאֲלוּ אַנְשֵׁי הַמָּקוֹם לְאִשְׁתּוֹ וַיֹּאמֶר אֲחֹתִי הִוא כִּי יָרֵא לֵאמֹר אִשְׁתִּי פֶּן יַהַרְגֻנִי אַנְשֵׁי הַמָּקוֹם עַל רִבְקָה כִּי טוֹבַת מַרְאֶה הִוא:

And Isaac dwelt in Gerar.

And the men of the place asked about his wife, and he said, "She is my sister," because he was afraid to say, "[She is] my wife," [because he said,] "Lest the men of the place kill me because of Rebecca, for she is of beautiful appearance."

TEXT 3A

Bereishit (Genesis) 50:15–17

וַיִּרְאוּ אֲחֵי יוֹסֵף כִּי מֵת אֲבִיהֶם וַיֹּאמְרוּ לוּ יִשְׂטְמֵנוּ יוֹסֵף וְהָשֵׁב יָשִׁיב לָנוּ
אֵת כָּל הָרָעָה אֲשֶׁר גָּמַלְנוּ אֹתוֹ:

וַיְצַוּוּ אֶל יוֹסֵף לֵאמֹר אָבִיךְ צִוָּה לִפְנֵי מוֹתוֹ לֵאמֹר:

כֹּה תֹאמְרוּ לְיוֹסֵף אָנָּא שָׂא נָא פֶּשַׁע אַחֶיךָ וְחַטָּאתָם כִּי רָעָה גְמָלוּךְ וְעַתָּה
שָׂא נָא לְפֶשַׁע עַבְדֵי אֱלֹקֵי אָבִיךְ וַיֵּבְךְּ יוֹסֵף בְּדַבְּרָם אֵלָיו:

Now, Joseph's brothers saw that their father had died, and they said, "Perhaps Joseph will hate us and return to us all the evil that we did to him."

So they commanded [messengers to go] to Joseph, to say, "Your father commanded [us] before his death, saying.

"'So shall you say to Joseph, "Please, forgive now your brothers' transgression and their sin, for they did evil to you. Now, please forgive the transgression of the *servants of the G-d of your father.'" Joseph wept when they spoke to him.*

TEXT 3B

Nachmanides, Pirush Haramban, Bereishit 45:27

יראה לי על דרך הפשט שלא הוגד ליעקב כל ימיו כי אחיו מכרו את יוסף, אבל
חשב כי היה תועה בשדה והמוצאים אותו לקחוהו ומכרו אותו אל מצרים.
כי אחיו לא רצו להגיד לו חטאתם, אף כי יראו לנפשם פן יקצוף ויקללם,
כאשר עשה בראובן ושמעון ולוי. ויוסף במוסרו הטוב לא רצה להגיד לו.
ולכך נאמר ויצוו אל יוסף לאמר אביך ציווה לפני מותו לאמר וגו', ואלו
ידע יעקב בענין הזה היה ראוי להם שיחלו פני אביהם במותו לצוות את
יוסף מפיו כי ישא פניו ולא ימרה את דברו, ולא היו בסכנה ולא יצטרכו
לבדות מלבם דברים.

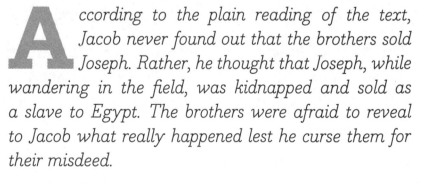

Rabbi Moshe Ben Nachaman
(Nachmanides, Ramban)
1194–1270

Scholar, philosopher, author and physician. Nachmanides was born in Spain and served as leader of Iberian Jewry. In 1263, he was summoned by King James of Aragon to a public disputation with Pablo Cristiani, a Jewish apostate. Though Nachmanides was the clear victor of the debate, he had to flee Spain because of the resulting persecution. He moved to Israel and helped reestablish communal life in Jerusalem. He authored a classic commentary on the Pentateuch and a commentary on the Talmud.

*A*ccording to the plain reading of the text, Jacob never found out that the brothers sold Joseph. Rather, he thought that Joseph, while wandering in the field, was kidnapped and sold as a slave to Egypt. The brothers were afraid to reveal to Jacob what really happened lest he curse them for their misdeed.

This is also evident from the fact that the brothers told Joseph that their father commanded them to tell him the message, and that Jacob himself didn't command Joseph—for Jacob never knew of the story.

Jacob Pulls the Wool over Esau's Eyes

TEXT 4A

Bereishit (Genesis) 27:15–19

וַתִּקַּח רִבְקָה אֶת בִּגְדֵי עֵשָׂו בְּנָהּ הַגָּדֹל הַחֲמֻדֹת אֲשֶׁר אִתָּהּ בַּבָּיִת וַתַּלְבֵּשׁ אֶת יַעֲקֹב בְּנָהּ הַקָּטָן:

וְאֵת עֹרֹת גְּדָיֵי הָעִזִּים הִלְבִּישָׁה עַל יָדָיו וְעַל חֶלְקַת צַוָּארָיו:

וַתִּתֵּן אֶת הַמַּטְעַמִּים וְאֶת הַלֶּחֶם אֲשֶׁר עָשָׂתָה בְּיַד יַעֲקֹב בְּנָהּ:

וַיָּבֹא אֶל אָבִיו וַיֹּאמֶר אָבִי וַיֹּאמֶר הִנֶּנִּי מִי אַתָּה בְּנִי:

וַיֹּאמֶר יַעֲקֹב אֶל אָבִיו אָנֹכִי עֵשָׂו בְּכֹרֶךָ עָשִׂיתִי כַּאֲשֶׁר דִּבַּרְתָּ אֵלָי קוּם נָא שְׁבָה וְאָכְלָה מִצֵּידִי בַּעֲבוּר תְּבָרֲכַנִּי נַפְשֶׁךָ:

And Rebecca took the costly garments of Esau, her elder son, which were with her in the house, and she dressed Jacob, her younger son.

And the hides of the kids she put on his hands and on the smoothness of his neck.

And she gave the tasty foods and the bread that she had made into the hand of Jacob her son.

And he came to his father and said, "My father!" And he said, "Here I am. Who are you, my son?"

And Jacob said to his father, "I am Esau, your first-born. I have done as you have spoken to me. Please rise, sit down, and eat of my game so that your soul will bless me."

TEXT 4B

Ibid., 27–35

וַיֹּאמֶר בָּא אָחִיךָ בְּמִרְמָה וַיִּקַּח בִּרְכָתֶךָ:

And he said, *"Your brother came with trickery and took your blessing."*

Question: What Was Rivkah Thinking?

TEXT 5

Rabbi Shalom Dovber Schneersohn (Rashab)
1860–1920

Chasidic rebbe. Rabbi Shalom Dovber became the fifth leader of the Chabad movement upon the passing of his father, Rabbi Shmuel of Lubavitch. He established the Lubavitch network of *yeshivot* called Tomchei Temimim. He authored many volumes of chasidic discourses and is renowned for his lucid and thorough explanations of kabbalistic concepts.

Rabbi Shalom Dovber of Lubavitch, The Rebbe Rashab, Sefer Hama'amarim, 5668, p. 65

הנה רבקה ויעקב עשו כמה ענייני רמאות ליקח את הברכות, במה שהלבישה את יעקב בבגדי עשו החמודות כו' ויעקב אמר אנכי עשו בכורך כו'. ולכאורה מפני מה הייתה ההנהגה באופן כזה, דלקיחת הברכות תהיה במרמה דווקא?

Rebecca and Jacob acted in a crooked manner, dressing Jacob in Esau's clothes and pretending to be Esau. Why was all this necessary? Why did it have to be that the firstborn blessings should come in such a crooked way?

Suffering the Consequences

TEXT 6A

Midrash Tanchuma Yashan, Vayetze §11

כל הלילה הייתה עושה עצמה כרחל, כיון שעמד בבוקר "והנה היא
לאה", אמר לה: בת הרמאי, למה רימית אותי?

אמרה לו: ואתה למה רימית אביך?! כשאמר לך, "האתה זה בני עשו?"
אמרת לו "אנכי עשו בכורך"—ואתה אומר "למה רימיתני?!"

The entire wedding night, Leah pretended she was Rachel. In the morning, Jacob realized that it was in fact Leah, so he asked her, "Why did you deceive me?"

Leah countered him asking, "Why did you deceive your father when you pretended to be Esau? And now you dare ask 'Why did you deceive me?!'"

Midrash Tanchuma

A midrashic work bearing the name of Rabbi Tanchuma, a 4th- century Talmudic sage quoted often in this work. Midrash is the designation of a particular genre of rabbinic literature usually forming a running commentary on specific books of the Bible. *Midrash Tanchuma* provides textual exegeses, expounds upon the biblical narrative, and develops and illustrates moral principles. *Tanchuma* is unique in that many of its sections commence with a halachic discussion, which subsequently leads into non-halachic teachings.

TEXT 6B

Rabbi Yaakov Baal Haturim, Bereishit 27:35

"ויענו בני יעקב את שכם... במרמה". הוא בא לאביו במרמה ובאו
בניו במרמה.

The verse states,] "And the children of Jacob acted with cunning." Jacob approached his father cunningly, so his own sons approached him cunningly.

Rabbi Yaakov Ben Asher
(Tur, Baal Haturim)
ca. 1269–1343

Halachic authority and codifier. Rabbi Ya'akov was born in Germany and moved to Toledo, Spain, with his father, the noted halachist Rabbeinu Asher, to escape persecution. He wrote *Arba'ah Turim*, an ingeniously organized and highly influential code of Jewish law. He is considered one of the greatest authorities of Halachah.

From a Halachic Perspective

A Beautiful Bride

TEXT 7

Talmud Tractate Ketubot, 16b

תנו רבנן: כיצד מרקדין לפני הכלה (מה אומרים לפניה. –רש"י): בית שמאי אומרים כלה כמות שהיא, ובית הלל אומרים כלה נאה וחסודה. אמרו להן בית שמאי לבית הלל הרי שהיתה חיגרת או סומא אומרים לה כלה נאה וחסודה—והתורה אמרה מדבר שקר תרחק? אמרו להם בית הלל לבית שמאי, לדבריכם, מי שלקח מקח רע מן השוק ישבחנו בעיניו או יגננו בעיניו? הוי אומר ישבחנו בעיניו. מכאן אמרו חכמים לעולם תהא דעתו של אדם מעורבת עם הבריות.

Babylonian Talmud
A literary work of monumental proportions that draws upon the legal, spiritual, intellectual, ethical, and historical traditions of Judaism. The 37 tractates of the Babylonian Talmud contain the teachings of the Jewish sages from the period after the destruction of the 2nd Temple through the 5th century CE. It has served as the primary vehicle for the transmission of the Oral Law and the education of Jews over the centuries; it is the entry point for all subsequent legal, ethical, and theological Jewish scholarship.

ur rabbis taught: How does one dance before the bride? (What do you tell her? –Rashi)

Beit Shammai say: The bride as she is. And Beit Hillel say, "A beautiful and graceful bride!"

Beit Shammai said to Beit Hillel: If she was lame or blind, does one say of her, "Beautiful and graceful bride?" The Torah says, "Keep away from a lie"?!

Beit Hillel said to Beit Shammai: According to your words, if one has made a bad purchase in the market, should one praise it in front of him or denigrate it? Surely, one should praise it in front of him!

Therefore, the Sages said: One should always have a pleasing disposition in front of other people.

The Ruling

TEXT 8

Talmud Tractate Yevamot, 65b

ואמר רבי אילעא משום רבי אלעזר ברבי שמעון מותר לו לאדם לשנות בדבר השלום שנאמר "אביך צוה וגו' כה תאמרו ליוסף אנא שא נא וגו'".

רבי נתן אומר: מצוה, שנאמר "ויאמר שמואל איך אלך ושמע שאול והרגני וגו'.

דבי רבי ישמעאל תנא: גדול השלום שאף הקדוש ברוך הוא שינה בו, דמעיקרא כתיב "ואדוני זקן", ולבסוף כתיב "ואני זקנתי".

Rabbi Ilea said in the name of Rabbi Elazar ben Rabbi Shimon: A person may edit what has been said for the sake of peace, as Joseph's brothers said, "Your father commanded … please forgive."

Rabbi Natan says, indeed, this is a commandment, as it is written "Samuel said, 'How can I go? If Saul hears it he will kill me.'"

The school of Rabbi Yishmael taught: Peace is so important that even G-d altered what was said for its sake! For at first, [Sarah says,] "My husband is old," and afterwards, [when G-d repeats her words to Abraham,] it says, "I am old."

TEXT 9

Shulchan Aruch, Yoreh Dei'ah 338

שולחן ערוך יורה דעה סימן שלח: מי שחלה ונוטה למות, אומרים לו: התוודה על מעשיך: בשכר שאתה מתוודה—אתה חי.

If one is deathly ill we tell him, "Repent for your past actions, and that alone should stand you in good stead for long life," [to calm him down, even though we know that it is very likely he is going to die].

The Truth/Peace Dilemma

Not Untrue

TEXT 10

Rabbi Eliezer ben Shmuel, Sefer Yeraim, ch. 235

כלומר, להתרחק מכל שקר שיוכל לבוא לידי היזק חברו או רעה לו...
אבל שקר שאינו בא לידי רעה, לא הזהירה התורה עליו.
דבר הלמד מעניינו הוא שהכתוב מדבר רק ברשע רע לבריות, דכתיב
"מדבר שקר תרחק ונקי צדיק אל תהרוג כי לא אצדיק רשע".

When the Torah says, "Keep away from a lie," the intent is to keep away from lies which can harm or hurt someone else. However, lies that do not lead to negativity are not included in the Torah's proscription.

This is understood from the context of the verse that states, "Distance yourself from words of falsehood; do not kill an innocent or righteous man."

Peace Is Superior

TEXT 11

Rabbi Yonah of Gerona
d. 1263

Spanish rabbi and Talmudist. Rabbeinu Yonah from Gerona, Catalonia, was a cousin of Nachmanides. He is renowned for his outspoken critique of Maimonides' works, and for later recanting his opposition and vowing to travel to Maimonides' grave in Israel to beg his forgiveness. He left France, but was detained in Toledo, Spain, where he stayed and became one of the greatest Talmudists of his time. He is best known for his moralistic works on repentance and asceticism.

Rabeinu Yonah, Avot, ch. 1

אמרו חכמינו ז"ל שאפילו ספור דברים בעלמא אין לו לאדם לשקר כההוא עובדא דבריה דרב וכו'... כי האדם המרגיל לשונו לדבר שקר בדבר שאין בה לא הפסד ולא תועלת, גם כי יבא לדבר דברים של עיקר לא יוכל לומר האמת כי פיהו המדבר וההרגל שולט עליו.

The Sages tell us that even when simply re-counting an event, it should be said truthfully, for when a person accustoms himself to lying, he will not be able to say the truth because he is so used to lying.

TXT 12

Talmud Tractate Yevamot, 63b

רב הוה קא מצערא ליה דביתהו כי אמר לה עבידי לי טלופחי עבדא ליה חימצי חימצי עבדא ליה טלופחי כי גדל חייא בריה אפיך לה אמר ליה איעליא לך אמך אמר ליה אנא הוא דקא אפיכנא לה אמר ליה היינו דקא אמרי אינשי דנפיק מינך טעמא מלפך את לא תעביד הכי שנאמר למדו לשונם דבר שקר.

Rav was constantly tormented by his wife. If he told her, "Prepare me lentils," she would prepare him small peas; [and if he asked for] small peas, she prepared him lentils.

When his son Chiya grew up, he gave her [his father's instruction] in the reverse order. "Your mother," Rav once remarked to him, "has improved!" "It was I," the other replied, "who reversed [your orders] to her."

"This is what people say," Rav said to him. "Your own offspring teaches you reason; you, however, must not continue to do so, for it is said, 'They have taught their tongue to speak lies, they weary themselves, etc.'"

TEXT 13

Midrash Bereishit Rabah 8:5

Bereishit Rabah
An early rabbinic commentary on the Book of Genesis. This Midrash bears the name of Rabbi Oshiya Rabah (Rabbi Oshiya "the Great") whose teaching opens this work. This Midrash provides textual exegeses and stories, expounds upon the biblical narrative, and develops and illustrates moral principles. Produced by the sages of the Talmud in the Land of Israel, its use of Aramaic closely resembles that of the Jerusalem Talmud. It was first printed in Constantinople in 1512 together with four other Midrashic works on the other four books of the Pentateuch.

בשעה שבא הקדוש ברוך הוא לבראות את אדם הראשון נעשו מלאכי השרת כיתים כיתים וחבורות חבורות מהם אומרים "אל יברא", ומהם אומרים "יברא", הדא הוא דכתיב "חסד ואמת נפגשו צדק ושלום נשקו". חסד אומר יברא שהוא גומל חסדים, ואמת אומר אל יברא שכולו שקרים...

מה עשה הקדוש ברוך הוא? נטל אמת והשליכו לארץ, הדא הוא דכתיב "ותשלך אמת ארצה".

When G-d set out to create man, there was a tumult in the Heavens. Some of the angels said, "Do not create man!" while others said "Create man!" This is what the verse is referring to when it says, "Truth will sprout from the earth, and righteousness will look down from heaven." Kindness said, "Create man for he will perform acts of kindness." Truth said "Do not create man for they are full of lies."

What did G-d do? He took hold of truth and flung him to the ground. This is what the verse is referring to when it says, "And Truth was thrown to the ground."

Truth Is Still Important

TEXT 14

Talmud Tractate Berachot 19b

גדול כבוד הבריות שדוחה לא תעשה שבתורה... כיצד אם היה כהן והיא בבית הקברות או היה זקן ואינה לפי כבודו... לכך נאמר "והתעלמת".

Great is the duty of honoring one's fellow creatures, since it sets aside a prohibition enjoined by the Torah. [The verse states,] "And hide yourself from them," [i.e., there are times when you may hide yourself from them, and times when you must not hide yourself from them.]

How can this be? If he was a Kohen and [the straying animal] was in a cemetery, or he was an Elder and it was derogatory to his dignity [to be seen leading the animal back], or his work was more important than his neighbor's. Therefore, it is stated, "And hide yourself."

STORY

A short story that powerfully illustrates the sometime-positive aspects of lying:

Two men, both seriously ill, occupied the same hospital room. One man was allowed to sit up in his bed for an hour each afternoon to receive his daily medical treatment. His bed was next to the room's only window. The other man had to spend all his time flat on his back. The men talked for hours on end. They spoke of their wives and families, their homes, their jobs, their involvement in the military service, and where they had been on vacation.

Every afternoon, when the man in the bed by the window could sit up, he would pass the time by describing to his roommate all the things he could see outside the window. The man in the other bed began to live for those one-hour periods when his world would be broadened and enlivened by the description of activity and color of the world outside.

The man by the window regaled his roommate, recounting that they overlooked a park with a beautiful lake. Ducks and swans played on the water while children sailed their model boats. Young lovers held hands and walked amidst flowers of every color of the rainbow. Grand old trees graced the landscape, and a fine view of the city skyline could be seen in the distance. As the man described his view from the window in exquisite detail, the man on the other side of the room would close his eyes and imagine the picturesque scene.

One warm afternoon, the man by the window described a parade passing through the park. Although the other man could not hear the band, he could see the parade in his mind's eye as the gentleman by the window developed a detailed picture with his descriptive words.

One morning, the nurse arrived to bring water for their baths only to find the lifeless body of the man by the window, who had died peacefully in his sleep. She was saddened and called the hospital attendants to take the body away.

As soon as it seemed appropriate, the other man asked if he could be moved next to the window. The nurse was happy to make the switch, and after making sure he was comfortable, she left him alone. Slowly, painfully, he propped himself up on one elbow to take his first look at the world outside. Finally, he would have the joy of seeing it for himself. He strained to slowly turn to look out the window beside the bed. To his surprise, the window faced a brick wall.

Revisiting the Forefathers

TEXT 15

Talmud Tractate Yevamot, op cit.

מותר לו לאדם לשנות בדבר השלום, שנאמר "אביך צוה וגו כה תאמרו ליוסף אנא שא נא וגו'".

ne is permitted to change the truth for the sake of peace, as we see from the story of the brothers lying to Joseph.

The Case of the Pidyon Haben

TEXT 16

Sha'alot U'Teshuvot Yabia Omer, op. cit.

איסור ברכה שאינה צריכה אינה אלא איסור מדרבנן... לכן טוב שלא
לגלות לו ולא כלום כדי שלא לגרום חשש גירושין בין בני הזוג ועל
כל פנים ודאי שיהיו מריבה וקטטה וביטול שלום הבית וגם בזיון גדול
לאישה ומשפחתה... הלכך יניחו לאב לעשות הפדיון עם שתי הברכות,
שגדול כבוד הברית שדוחה לא תעשה שבתורה.

The prohibition of making a blessing in vain is of a Rabbinic nature... Therefore, better that she should remain silent so as not to create a situation of legitimate concern that the husband might look for a divorce, or at the very least there will be disharmony and fighting in the house, shaming the woman. Better to allow the father to perform the ceremony with the appropriate blessings, for "Great is human dignity that it even overrides biblical prohibitions."

The Journey to the Goal

Releasing Trapped Sparks

TEXT 17

Rabbi Menachem Mendel Schneerson
1902–1994

The towering Jewish leader of the 20th century, known as "the Lubavitcher Rebbe," or simply as "the Rebbe." Born in southern Ukraine, the Rebbe escaped Nazi-occupied Europe, arriving in the U.S. in June 1941. The Rebbe inspired and guided the revival of traditional Judaism after the European devastation, impacting virtually every Jewish community the world over. The Rebbe often emphasized that the performance of just one additional good deed could usher in the era of Moshiach. The Rebbe's scholarly talks and writings have been printed in more than 200 volumes.

The Lubavitcher Rebbe, Likutei Sichot, vol. 3, p. 795

בכדי לקבל את הברכות האלוקיות, רבקה עשתה כמה עניני רמיה ויעקב לבש את בגדי עשו (שהיו במקורם בגדי נמרוד, שהמריד את העולם כולו נגד ה').

ומכך ההוראה לכולנו: הגישה של יהודי לעניני העולם, היא באופן של רמאות: לכאורה הוא עסוק בעניני גשמיות, אכילה ושתיה וכך הלאה, אך הכוונה שלו בכך היא לשם שמים. הוא אמנם לובש את בגדי עשו, אבל הכוונה שלו בכך היא לגאול את ניצוצות הקדושה שנפלו שם.

To receive the blessings, Rebecca acted in cunning and Jacob dressed in Esau's clothes (which were originally Nimrod's clothing—a man who rallied all to rebel against G-d).

The lesson for us is clear: The approach of a Jew to mundane matters has to be one of cunning. On the surface, he is engaged in mundane affairs, eating, drinking, etc., but his real intention is for G-d's sake. Granted, he wears the clothes of Esau, but his **intention** is to refine the sparks of holiness that are to be found in the mundane.

Beating the Yetzer Hara at His Own Game

TEXT 18

The Lubavitcher Rebbe, Torat Menachem, 5711, p. 222

הטעם שברכות יצחק ליעקב היו צריכות לבוא בדרך "מרמה" דוקא,
לפי שנפילת ניצוצות הקדושה על ידי חטא עץ הדעת היתה במרמה,
כמו שכתוב "והנחש היה ערום", ולכן גם סדר העלאתם על ידי יעקב
(שהוא מעין אדם הראשון, כנאמר בגמרא שפניו של יעקב אבינו היו
דומות לפניו של אדם הראשון), שלקיחת הברכות מעשיו צריכה להיות
בדרך מרמה, כמו שכתוב "עם עקש תתפל".

The reason Isaac's blessings had to come about in a way of deceit specifically is because the sparks of holiness fell into this world through the sin of eating the forbidden fruits, something the snake orchestrated with slyness, as it is stated, "The snake was cunning."

Therefore, the way for Jacob to uplift these sparks was to receive the blessings from Isaac through slyness, as the verse says, "But with a perverse one, You deal crookedly."

STORY

Professor Velvel Green was a world-renowned scientist who had become an observant Jew. The Rebbe would send him on different lecture tours around the world to show that being a religious Jew is not contradictory to being very accomplished in the world of academia.

It happened once that he received an invitation to speak at a Conservative synagogue in Detroit, but upon looking up the Hebrew date in the calendar, he realized that it would fall out on the Jewish date of 19th of Kislev (a day of great importance in the Chabad calendar). His initial instinct was to postpone his speech so he would be able to spend this joyous day in Brooklyn together with the Rebbe. But reminding himself how much the Rebbe stressed the importance of these speeches, he didn't postpone the speech, consoling himself with the fact that after the speech he would go join the *farbrengen* in the local Chabad House.

After arriving in Detroit, Professor Green made contact with the Chabad House to find out when the *farbrengen* would be starting. Imagine his disappointment on finding out that Rabbi Shemtov, along with all the other Chabad rabbis in the area, had traveled to Brooklyn to be with the Rebbe in 770...

Feeling down, he wrote a letter to the Rebbe, complaining of how all the *shluchim* would be spending the 19th of Kislev with the Rebbe, and he would be stuck giving a speech in a Conservative synagogue.

He immediately received a reply from the Rebbe. "When you sit with Jews on the 19th of Kislev and talk with them about Judaism, you are closer to me than even those who are sitting around me at the *farbrengen*."

6

VAYETZE

The Nighttime Plea

Finding Hope in the Darkness

Dedicated in loving memory of Rabbi Yosef Yitzchok Shur

לע"נ הרה"ח המשפיע ר' יוסף יצחק בן הרה"ח ר' חיים שניאור זלמן שור | נפטר ר"ח מנחם אב ה'תשע"ו

PARASHA OVERVIEW
Vayetze

Jacob leaves his hometown of Beersheba and journeys to Charan. On the way, he encounters "the place" and sleeps there, dreaming of a ladder connecting heaven and earth, with angels climbing and descending on it; G-d appears and promises that the land upon which he lies will be given to his descendants. In the morning, Jacob raises the stone on which he laid his head as an altar and monument, pledging that it will be made the house of G-d.

In Haran, Jacob stays with and works for his uncle Laban, tending Laban's sheep. Laban agrees to give him his younger daughter, Rachel—whom Jacob loves—in marriage, in return for seven years' labor. But on the wedding night, Laban gives him his elder daughter, Leah, instead—a deception Jacob discovers only in the morning. Jacob marries Rachel, too, a week later, after agreeing to work another seven years for Laban.

Leah gives birth to six sons—Reuben, Simeon, Levi, Judah, Issachar and Zebulun—and a daughter, Dinah, while Rachel remains barren. Rachel gives Jacob her handmaid, Bilhah, as a wife to bear children in her stead, and two more sons, Dan and Naphtali, are born.

Leah does the same with her handmaid, Zilpah, who gives birth to Gad and Asher. Finally, Rachel's prayers are answered and she gives birth to Joseph.

Jacob has now been in Charan for fourteen years, and wishes to return home. But Laban persuades him to remain, now offering him sheep in return for his labor. Jacob prospers, despite Laban's repeated attempts to swindle him. After six years, Jacob leaves Charan in stealth, fearing that Laban would prevent him from leaving with the family and property for which he labored. Laban pursues Jacob, but is warned by G-d in a dream not to harm him. Laban and Jacob make a pact on Mount Gal-Ed, attested to by a pile of stones, and Jacob proceeds to the Holy Land, where he is met by angels.

The Origin of Prayer

Jacob's Prayer

TEXT 1A

Bereishit (Genesis) 28:10–11

וַיֵּצֵא יַעֲקֹב מִבְּאֵר שָׁבַע וַיֵּלֶךְ חָרָנָה:

וַיִּפְגַּע בַּמָּקוֹם וַיָּלֶן שָׁם כִּי בָא הַשֶּׁמֶשׁ וַיִּקַּח מֵאַבְנֵי הַמָּקוֹם וַיָּשֶׂם
מְרַאֲשֹׁתָיו וַיִּשְׁכַּב בַּמָּקוֹם הַהוּא:

And Jacob left Beer Sheba, and he went to Charan.

And he arrived at the place and lodged there because the sun had set, and he took some of the stones of the place and placed [them] at his head, and he lay down in that place.

TEXT 1B

Rashi, ad loc.

"וַיִּפְגַּע". כמו "וּפָגַע בִּירִיחוֹ", "וּפָגַע בְּדַבָּשֶׁת".

ורבותינו פירשו לשון תפלה כמו "וְאַל תִּפְגַּע בִּי", ולמדנו שתקן
תפלת ערבית.

"**A**nd he arrived." The Hebrew word "vayifga," as in "and it reached (u'faga) Jericho"; "And it reached (u'faga) Dabbesheth."

[Alternatively,] Our Rabbis interpreted [the word vayifga] as an expression of prayer, as in, "And do not entreat (tifga) me." This teaches us that he [Jacob] instituted the evening prayer.

Rabbi Shlomo Yitzchaki (Rashi)
1040–1105
Most noted biblical and Talmudic commentator. Born in Troyes, France, Rashi studied in the famed *yeshivot* of Mainz and Worms. His commentaries on the Pentateuch and the Talmud, which focus on the straightforward meaning of the text, appear in virtually every edition of the Talmud and Bible.

Original Orisons

TEXT 2A

Talmud Tractate Berachot, 26a–b

איתמר: רבי יוסי ברבי חנינא אומר תפלות אבות תקנום. רבי יהושע בן לוי אמר תפלות כנגד תמידין תקנום.

תניא כוותיה דרבי יוסי ברבי חנינא: אברהם תיקן תפלת שחרית, שנאמר "וישכם אברהם בבוקר אל המקום אשר עמד שם", ואין עמידה אלא תפלה, שנאמר "ויעמוד פנחס ויפלל".

יצחק תקן תפלת מנחה, שנאמר "ויצא יצחק לשוח בשדה לפנות ערב", ואין שיחה אלא תפלה, שנאמר "תפלה לעני כי יעטוף ולפני ה' ישפוך שיחו".

יעקב תקן תפלת ערבית, שנאמר "ויפגע במקום וילן שם" ואין פגיעה אלא תפלה", שנאמר "ואתה אל תתפלל בעד העם הזה ואל תשא בעדם רנה ותפלה ואל תפגע בי".

Babylonian Talmud
A literary work of monumental proportions that draws upon the legal, spiritual, intellectual, ethical, and historical traditions of Judaism. The 37 tractates of the Babylonian Talmud contain the teachings of the Jewish sages from the period after the destruction of the 2nd Temple through the 5th century CE. It has served as the primary vehicle for the transmission of the Oral Law and the education of Jews over the centuries; it is the entry point for all subsequent legal, ethical, and theological Jewish scholarship.

It has been stated: Rabbi Yose, son of Rabbi Chanina, said: The prayers were instituted by the Patriarchs…

It has been taught in accordance with Rabbi Yose ben Chanina: Abraham instituted the morning prayer, as it is stated, "And Abraham got up early in the morning to the place where he had stood"; "standing" means prayer, as it is said, "Then Pinchas stood up and prayed."

Isaac instituted the afternoon prayer, as it is stated, "And Isaac went out to meditate in the field at eventide"; "meditation" [sichah] means prayer, as it is stated, "A prayer of the afflicted when he faints and pours out his complaint [sichah] before G-d."

Jacob instituted the evening prayer, as it is stated, "And he arrived [paga] upon the place, and tarried there all night"; "arrived" means prayer, as it is stated, "Therefore pray not you for this people, neither lift up cry nor prayer for them, neither make intercession [paga] to Me."

Sacrificial Rite

TEXT 2B

Ibid.

רבי יהושע בן לוי אמר תפלות כנגד תמידין תקנום...
ותניא כוותיה דרבי יהושע בן לוי: מפני מה אמרו תפלת השחר עד
חצות שהרי תמיד של שחר קרב והולך עד חצות. ורבי יהודה אומר עד
ארבע שעות של שהרי תמיד של שחר קרב והולך עד ארבע שעות.
ומפני מה אמרו תפלת המנחה עד הערב שהרי תמיד של בין הערבים
קרב והולך עד הערב... ומפני מה אמרו תפלת הערב אין לה קבע שהרי
אברים ופדרים שלא נתעכלו מבערב קרבים והולכים כל הלילה ומפני
מה אמרו של מוספין כל היום שהרי קרבן של מוספין קרב כל היום.

Rabbi Yehoshua ben Levi says: The prayers were instituted to replace the daily sacrifices…

It has been taught also in accordance with Rabbi Yehoshua ben Levi: Why did they say that the morning prayer could be said till midday? Because the regular morning sacrifice could be brought up to midday…

And why did they say that the afternoon prayer can be said up to the evening? Because the regular afternoon offering can be brought up to the evening.

And why did they say that for the evening prayer there is no limit? Because the limbs and the fats that were not consumed [on the Altar] by the evening could be offered the entire night.

And why did they say that the additional [musaf] prayers could be said throughout the entire day? Because the additional [musaf] offering could be brought during the whole of the day.

Single Origin, or Double?

TEXT 2C

Ibid.

נימא תיהוי תיובתיה דרבי יוסי ברבי חנינא! אמר לך רבי יוסי ברברי חנינא לעולם אימא לך תפלות אבות תקנום ואסמכינהו רבנן אקרבנות. דאי לא תימא הכי, תפלת מוסף לרבי יוסי ברבי חנינא מאן תקנה? — אלא תפלות אבות תקנום, ואסמכינהו רבנן אקרבנות.

hall we say that this is a refutation of Rabbi Yose ben Chanina?

Rabbi Yose ben Chanina can answer: I can still maintain that the Patriarchs instituted the prayers, but the Rabbis found a basis for them in the offerings. For if you do not assume this, who, according to Rabbi Yose ben Chanina, instituted the additional [musaf] prayer? He must maintain, therefore, that the Patriarchs instituted the prayers and the Rabbis found a basis for them in the offerings.

TEXT 3A

Maimonides, Mishneh Torah, Laws of Kings 9:1

עַל שִׁשָּׁה דְּבָרִים נִצְטַוָּה אָדָם הָרִאשׁוֹן עַל עֲבוֹדָה זָרָה וְעַל בִּרְכַּת הַשֵּׁם וְעַל שְׁפִיכוּת דָּמִים וְעַל גִּלּוּי עֲרָיוֹת וְעַל הַגָּזֵל וְעַל הַדִּינִים... הוֹסִיף לְנֹחַ אֵבָר מִן הַחַי, שֶׁנֶּאֱמַר "אַךְ בָּשָׂר בְּנַפְשׁוֹ דָמוֹ לֹא תֹאכֵלוּ". נִמְצְאוּ שֶׁבַע מִצְוֺת.

וְכֵן הָיָה הַדָּבָר בְּכָל הָעוֹלָם עַד אַבְרָהָם. בָּא אַבְרָהָם וְנִצְטַוָּה יֶתֶר עַל אֵלוּ בְּמִילָה. וְהוּא הִתְפַּלֵּל שַׁחֲרִית. וְיִצְחָק הִפְרִישׁ מַעֲשֵׂר וְהוֹסִיף תְּפִלָּה אַחֶרֶת לִפְנוֹת הַיּוֹם. וְיַעֲקֹב הוֹסִיף גִּיד הַנָּשֶׁה וְהִתְפַּלֵּל עַרְבִית, עַד שֶׁבָּא מֹשֶׁה רַבֵּינוּ וְנִשְׁלְמָה תּוֹרָה עַל יָדוֹ.

Six precepts were commanded to Adam: a) the prohibition against worship of false gods; b) the prohibition against cursing G-d; c) the prohibition against murder; d) the prohibition against incest and adultery; e) the prohibition against theft; f) the command to establish laws and courts of justice... The prohibition against eating flesh from a living animal was added for Noah... Thus there are seven mitzvot.

These matters remained the same throughout the world until Abraham. When Abraham arose, in addition to these, he was commanded regarding circumcision. He also established the morning prayers.

Isaac separated tithes and established an additional prayer service before sunset.

Jacob added the prohibition against eating the sciatic nerve. He also established the evening prayers.

Rabbi Moshe ben Maimon (Maimonides, Rambam) 1135–1204

Halachist, philosopher, author, and physician. Maimonides was born in Cordoba, Spain. After the conquest of Cordoba by the Almohads, he fled Spain and eventually settled in Cairo, Egypt. There, he became the leader of the Jewish community and served as court physician to the vizier of Egypt. He is most noted for authoring the *Mishneh Torah*, an encyclopedic arrangement of Jewish law, and for his philosophical work, *Guide for the Perplexed*. His rulings on Jewish law are integral to the formation of halachic consensus.

In Egypt, Amram was commanded regarding other mitzvot. Ultimately, Moses came and the Torah was completed by him.

TEXT 3B

Ibid., Laws of Prayer, 1:5–6

וכן תקנו שיהא מנין התפלות כמנין הקרבנות, שתי תפלות בכל יום כנגד שני תמידין וכל יום שיש בו קרבן מוסף תקנו בו תפלה שלישית כנגד קרבן מוסף, ותפלה שהיא כנגד תמיד של בקר היא הנקראת תפלת השחר, ותפלה שכנגד תמיד של בין הערבים היא הנקראת תפלת מנחה ותפלה שכנגד המוספין היא נקראת תפלת המוספין.

וכן התקינו שיהא אדם מתפלל תפלה אחת בלילה שהרי איברי תמיד של בין הערבים מתעכלין והולכין כל הלילה שנאמר היא העולה וגו'.

They also decreed that the number of prayers correspond to the number of sacrifices... The prayer that corresponds to the daily morning sacrifice is called the Shacharit *Prayer. The prayer that corresponds to the daily sacrifice offered in the afternoon is called the* Minchah *Prayer and the prayer corresponding to the additional offerings is called the* Musaf *Prayer.*

They also instituted a prayer to be recited at night, since the limbs of the daily afternoon offering could be burned the whole night, as the verse states, "The burnt offering [shall remain on the Altar hearth all night until morning]."

The Need for the Patriarchs

TEXT 4

Rabbi Yom Tov Asevilli, Ritva to Berachot 26b

פירוש ודאי האבות תקנו, אבל מפני תקנתם לא היינו מחוייבים לאומרם.
אתו רבנן ואסמכינהו אקרבנות כדי שיהו חובה.

The meaning of this is as follows: Certainly, the Patriarchs instituted the prayers, but [on that basis alone] we would be under no obligation to follow their institution. The Rabbis then came along and based the institution on the sacrificial rite, so that it would be obligatory.

Rabbi Yomtov Asevilli (Ritva)
ca. 1250–1330
Spanish rabbi and Talmudist. Ritva was born in Seville. He is mostly known for his Talmudic commentary, which is extremely clear, and to this day, remains most frequently quoted and used.

TEXT 5

Midrash Shemot Rabah, 68:9

אמר רבי יהושע בן לוי: אבות הראשונים התקינו שלש תפלות.

abbi Yehoshua ben Levi said: The first Fathers instituted the three prayers.

Shemot Rabah
An early rabbinic commentary on the Book of Exodus. Midrash is the designation of a particular genre of rabbinic literature usually forming a running commentary on specific books of the Bible. *Shemot Rabah*, written mostly in Hebrew, provides textual exegeses, expounds upon the biblical narrative, and develops and illustrates moral principles. It was first printed in Constantinople in 1512 together with four other midrashic works on the other four books of the Pentateuch.

Third Is Different

The Need to Pray

TEXT 6

Maimonides, Laws of Prayer, 1:1

מצות עשה להתפלל בכל יום שנאמר "ועבדתם את ה' אלקיכם", מפי
השמועה למדו שעבודה זו היא תפלה, שנאמר "ולעבדו בכל לבבכם"—
אמרו חכמים "אי זו היא עבודה שבלב? –זו תפלה". ואין מנין התפלות
מן התורה, ואין משנה התפלה הזאת מן התורה, ואין לתפלה זמן קבוע
מן התורה.

It is a positive Torah commandment to pray every day, as it is stated, "You shall serve G-d, your G-d." Tradition teaches us that this service is prayer, as it is stated, "And serve Him with all your heart," and our Sages said, "Which is the service of the heart?—This is prayer."

The number of prayers is not prescribed in the Torah, nor does it prescribe a specific formula for prayer. Also, according to Torah law, there are no fixed times for prayers.

TEXT 7

Nachmanides, Glosses to Sefer Hamitzvot (Rambam) §5

ודאי כל עניין התפילה אינו חובה כלל, אבל הוא ממידת חסד הבורא
יתברך עלינו ששומע ועונה בכל קראנו אליו.

Certainly, the entire matter of prayer is not a
[biblical] obligation at all. Rather, it is a feature of the Blessed Creator's kindness toward
us, that He hears and answers whenever we call out
to Him.

Rabbi Moshe ben Nachman
(Nachmanides, Ramban)
1194–1270
Scholar, philosopher, author
and physician. Nachmanides
was born in Spain and served
as leader of Iberian Jewry. In
1263, he was summoned by
King James of Aragon to a
public disputation with Pablo
Cristiani, a Jewish apostate.
Though Nachmanides was the
clear victor of the debate, he
had to flee Spain because of
the resulting persecution. He
moved to Israel and helped
reestablish communal life
in Jerusalem. He authored
a classic commentary
on the Pentateuch and a
commentary on the Talmud.

Optional Evening Prayer

TEXT 8

Maimonides, Laws of Prayer 1:6

ואין תפלת ערבית חובה כתפלת שחרית ומנחה, ואף על פי כן נהגו
כל ישראל בכל מקומות מושבותיהם להתפלל ערבית וקבלוה עליהם
כתפלת חובה.

The Evening Prayer is not obligatory as are the
morning and afternoon prayers. Nevertheless,
the Jewish people, in all the places that they
have settled, are accustomed to recite the Evening
Prayer and have accepted it upon themselves as an
obligatory prayer.

Three Models

Sunrise

TEXT 9

Talmud Tractate Baba Batra, 15b

רבי אליעזר המודעי אומר איצטגנינות היתה בלבו של אברהם אבינו
שכל מלכי מזרח ומערב משכימין לפתחו (ליטול עצה הימנו –רש"י).

Rabbi Eliezer the Modiite said that Abraham possessed a power of reading the stars, for which he was much sought after by the kings of the East and West (to take advice from him —Rashi).

The Shadows Lengthen

TEXT 10A

Bereishit (Genesis) 25:11

וַיְהִי אַחֲרֵי מוֹת אַבְרָהָם וַיְבָרֶךְ אֱלֹקִים אֶת יִצְחָק בְּנוֹ וַיֵּשֶׁב יִצְחָק עִם בְּאֵר
לַחַי רֹאִי:

Now, it came to pass after Abraham's death that G-d blessed his son Isaac, and Isaac dwelt near Be'er Lachai Ro'i.

TEXT 10B

Rashi, ad loc.

דבר אחר אף על פי שמסר הקדוש ברוך הוא את הברכות לאברהם,
נתיירא לברך את יצחק מפני שצפה את עשו יוצא ממנו, אמר יבא בעל
הברכות ויברך את אשר ייטב בעיניו ובא הקדוש ברוך הוא וברכו:

"Now it came to pass after Abraham's death, that G-d blessed, etc."… Another explanation: Even though the Holy One, blessed be He, delivered the blessings to Abraham, he was afraid to bless Isaac because he foresaw Esau emanating from him. So, he said, "May the Master of blessings come and bless whomever He pleases." And the Holy One, blessed be He, came and blessed him.

Dusk

TEXT 11

Rabbi Chaim ibn Attar, Ohr HaChayim, Bereishit 28:13

ובדרך רמז כל הפרשה תרמוז ענין האדם וכמו שהתחילו לומר בה
רבותינו ז"ל: ויצא יעקב הוא הנפש בצאתה מעולם העליון ונקרא יעקב
על שם יצר הרע הכרוך בעקביו. ואומרו מבאר שבע מקום שממנו יצאו
הנשמות יקרא באר מים חיים, ושבע ירמוז אל שבועת ה' אשר תשבע
הנפש בצאתה שלא תעבור על דבר תורה...
ואומר ויפגע במקום כי צריך האדם להתפלל לה' שהוא מקומו של עולם
שלא יעזבנו בידו. ואומר וילן שם כי בא השמש שצריך להתנהג כן עד לכתו
מעולם הזה כשיעריב שמשו, והוא אומר ז"ל אל תאמין בעצמך עד יום מותך...

ואחר כל התנאים הללו מובטח הוא שינצח היצר הרע. ומעתה מבשרו הכתוב שיהיה ראוי לענף מענפי הנבואה שיגלה ה' אליו בחלום ידבר בו.

Rabbi Chayim ibn Atar
(Or Hachayim)
1696–1743
Biblical exegete, kabbalist, and Talmudist. Rabbi Atar, born in Meknes, Morocco, was a prominent member of the Moroccan rabbinate and later immigrated to the Land of Israel. He is most famous for his *Or Hachayim*, a popular commentary on the Torah. The famed Jewish historian and bibliophile Rabbi Chaim Yosef David Azulai was among his most notable disciples.

In an allegorical sense, this entire chapter alludes to the matter of man. Our Sages first said of the verse "And Jacob departed from Be'er-sheva, and he went to Haran," that [this departure] alludes to the soul's departure from the Upper World; [the name Yaakov is an allusion to] the Evil Inclination that is bound to man's heel (ekev) [from the moment of his birth]; they have said that Be'er-Sheva [is a reference to the] place from which the souls emerge, which is the well [be'er] of living water; "sheva" alludes to the oath [shavua] that the soul makes with G-d as it emerges, not to violate the words of the Torah…

It says that "he encountered that place" [which is a reference to prayer] because man must pray to G-d, the [Omnipresent], who is "the place of the world," that He does not leave him. It continues to say, "And he lodged there for the sun had set," because one must conduct himself in this manner of active service until his sun sets, as the Sages have said, "Do not rely on yourself until the day you die"…

After all of these conditions, one can be confident that he will defeat the Evil Inclination, and now Scripture informs [the reader] that he can be worthy of an offshoot of prophecy, that G-d will reveal Himself to him, and speak to him in a dream [as He did with Jacob]…

Song for Myself

TEXT 12

The Lubavitcher Rebbe, Likutei Sichot, vol. 15, p. 246

אײנע פון די מעלות אין עבודת התשובה (כפשוטה) איז, וואס תשובה
ברענגט ארויס דעם תוקף פון דער התקשרות פון א אידן מיטן
אויבערשטן, אז די התקשרות פארלירט זיך ניט ח״ו אפילו דורך א חטא
און וואס דערפאר קען ער אפילו לאחרי החטא נאך אלץ תשובה טאן.
ועל דרך זה איז אויך בנוגע דעם ענין ה"תשובה" וואס איז דא אין דער
עבודת הנשמה בירידתה למטה אז אין דעם זאגט זיך ארויס בגילוי דער
תוקף ההתקשרות פון דער נשמה מיטן אויבערשטן אז אויך ווען זי איז
אנגעטאן אין גוף ונפש הבהמית (און יצר הרע) איז זי פארבונדן מיטן
אויבערשטן דורך עבודת ה'.

Rabbi Menachem Mendel Schneerson
1902–1994
The towering Jewish leader of the 20th century, known as "the Lubavitcher Rebbe," or simply as "the Rebbe." Born in southern Ukraine, the Rebbe escaped Nazi-occupied Europe, arriving in the U.S. in June 1941. The Rebbe inspired and guided the revival of traditional Judaism after the European devastation, impacting virtually every Jewish community the world over. The Rebbe often emphasized that the performance of just one additional good deed could usher in the era of Moshiach. The Rebbe's scholarly talks and writings have been printed in more than 200 volumes.

One of the characteristics of teshuvah *is that repentance and returning to G-d bring out the power of the bond a Jew shares with G-d. It is because this connection can never be lost, even by sin, that one can always perform* teshuvah *and return to G-d, even after committing a sin, Heaven forbid.*

So it is with the "teshuvah" that the soul must accomplish when it descends below. Through it the soul's powerful bond with G-d becomes manifest, such that even when it is clothed inside a body and the animal soul (and the Evil Inclination), it can remain connected with G-d in its service of the Divine.

TEXT 13

Midrash, Bereishit Rabah 68:11

"וישכב במקום ההוא". רבי יהודה ורבי נחמיה. רבי יהודה אמר: כאן שכב, אבל כל י"ד שנה, שהיה טמון בבית עבר לא שכב. רבי נחמיה אמר: כאן שכב, אבל כל כ' שנה, שעמד בביתו של לבן, לא שכב. ומה היה אומר? רבי יהושע בן לוי אמר: ט"ו שיר המעלות שבספר תהלים. מאי טעמיה? "שיר המעלות לדוד, לולי ה' שהיה לנו יאמר נא ישראל", ישראל סבא.

Bereishit Rabah

An early rabbinic commentary on the Book of Genesis. This Midrash bears the name of Rabbi Oshiya Rabah (Rabbi Oshiya "the Great") whose teaching opens this work. This Midrash provides textual exegeses and stories, expounds upon the biblical narrative, and develops and illustrates moral principles. Produced by the sages of the Talmud in the Land of Israel, its use of Aramaic closely resembles that of the Jerusalem Talmud. It was first printed in Constantinople in 1512 together with four other Midrashic works on the other four books of the Pentateuch.

"And lay down in that place..." Rabbi Yehuda and Rabbi Nechemiah [both understand this verse to imply an inverse proposition]: Rabbi Yehuda says that he lay here, but for the entire 14 years that he spent hiding in the [Study] House of Ever he did not lie [down to sleep]. Rabbi Nechemiah said that he lay here, but for the entire 20 years he remained in Lavan's house he did not lie.

And what would he say [throughout his stay in Lavan's house]?

Rabbi Yehoshua ben Levi said [he would recite] the 15 Psalms of the Book of Tehillim [from 120–134, beginning with the words] "A song of ascents." What is his reason [for proposing this? Because of the opening lines of Psalm 124,] "A song of ascents, from David. Were it not for G-d, Who was on our side, let Israel now declare..." "Israel" refers to the elder Israel [i.e. Yaakov].

7

Culpable or Collateral?

The Destruction of Shechem

Dedicated in loving memory of Mr. Alfons Weber

לע״נ אהרן יחזקאל בן אברהם ולינה

PARASHA OVERVIEW
Vayishlach

Jacob returns to the Holy Land after a 20-year stay in Charan, and sends angel-emissaries to Esau in hope of a reconciliation, but his messengers report that his brother is on the warpath with 400 armed men. Jacob prepares for war, prays, and sends Esau a large gift (consisting of hundreds of heads of livestock) to appease him.

That night, Jacob ferries his family and possessions across the Jabbok River; he, however, remains behind and encounters the angel that embodies the spirit of Esau, with whom he wrestles until daybreak. Jacob suffers a dislocated hip but vanquishes the supernal creature, who bestows on him the name Israel, which means "he who prevails over the divine."

Jacob and Esau meet, embrace and kiss, but part ways. Jacob purchases a plot of land near Shechem, whose crown prince—also called Shechem—abducts and rapes Jacob's daughter Dinah. Dinah's brothers Simeon and Levi avenge the deed by killing all male inhabitants of the city, after rendering them vulnerable by convincing them to circumcise themselves.

Jacob journeys on. Rachel dies while giving birth to her second son, Benjamin, and is buried in a roadside grave near Bethlehem. Reuben loses the birthright because he interferes with his father's marital life. Jacob arrives in Hebron, to his father Isaac, who later dies at age 180. (Rebecca has passed away before Jacob's arrival.)

Our Parshah concludes with a detailed account of Esau's wives, children and grandchildren; the family histories of the people of Seir, among whom Esau settled; and a list of the eight kings who ruled Edom, the land of Esau's and Seir's descendants.

The Shechem Saga

Dinah and Shechem

TEXT 1A

Bereishit (Genesis) 34:1–4

וַתֵּצֵא דִינָה בַּת לֵאָה אֲשֶׁר יָלְדָה לְיַעֲקֹב לִרְאוֹת בִּבְנוֹת הָאָרֶץ:

וַיַּרְא אֹתָהּ שְׁכֶם בֶּן חֲמוֹר הַחִוִּי נְשִׂיא הָאָרֶץ וַיִּקַּח אֹתָהּ וַיִּשְׁכַּב אֹתָהּ וַיְעַנֶּהָ:...

וַיֹּאמֶר שְׁכֶם אֶל חֲמוֹר אָבִיו לֵאמֹר קַח לִי אֶת הַיַּלְדָּה הַזֹּאת לְאִשָּׁה:

inah, the daughter of Leah, whom she had borne to Jacob, went out to look about among the daughters of the land.

And Shechem, the son of Hamor, the Hivvite, the prince of the land, saw her, and he took her, lay with her, and violated her...

And Shechem spoke to his father, Hamor, saying, "Take this girl for me as a wife."

TEXT 1B

Ibid., 34:13–15, 24–25

וַיַּעֲנוּ בְנֵי יַעֲקֹב אֶת שְׁכֶם וְאֶת חֲמוֹר אָבִיו בְּמִרְמָה וַיְדַבֵּרוּ אֲשֶׁר טִמֵּא אֵת דִּינָה אֲחֹתָם:

וַיֹּאמְרוּ אֲלֵיהֶם לֹא נוּכַל לַעֲשׂוֹת הַדָּבָר הַזֶּה לָתֵת אֶת אֲחֹתֵנוּ לְאִישׁ אֲשֶׁר לוֹ עָרְלָה כִּי חֶרְפָּה הִוא לָנוּ:

אַךְ־בְּזֹאת, נֵאוֹת לָכֶם: אִם תִּהְיוּ כָמֹנוּ, לְהִמֹּל לָכֶם כָּל־זָכָר...

וַיִּשְׁמְעוּ אֶל חֲמוֹר וְאֶל שְׁכֶם בְּנוֹ כָּל יֹצְאֵי שַׁעַר עִירוֹ וַיִּמֹּלוּ כָּל זָכָר כָּל יֹצְאֵי שַׁעַר עִירוֹ:

וַיְהִי בַיּוֹם הַשְּׁלִישִׁי בִּהְיוֹתָם כֹּאֲבִים וַיִּקְחוּ שְׁנֵי בְנֵי יַעֲקֹב שִׁמְעוֹן וְלֵוִי אֲחֵי דִינָה אִישׁ חַרְבּוֹ וַיָּבֹאוּ עַל הָעִיר בֶּטַח וַיַּהַרְגוּ כָּל זָכָר:

Thereupon, Jacob's sons answered Shechem and his father Hamor with cunning, and they spoke, because [after all] he had defiled their sister Dinah.

"We cannot do this thing, to give our sister to a man who has a foreskin, for that is a disgrace to us. But with this, however, we will consent to you, if you will be like us, that every male will be circumcised…"

And all those coming out of the gate of his city listened to Hamor and his son Shechem, and every male, all who go out of the gate of his city, became circumcised.

Now, it came to pass on the third day, when they were in pain, that Jacob's two sons, Shimon and Levi, Dinah's brothers, each took his sword, and they came upon the city with confidence, and they slew every male.

An Intractable Problem?

TEXT 2

Rabbi Moshe ben Nachman
(Nachmanides, Ramban)
1194–1270

Scholar, philosopher, author and physician. Nachmanides was born in Spain and served as leader of Iberian Jewry. In 1263, he was summoned by King James of Aragon to a public disputation with Pablo Cristiani, a Jewish apostate. Though Nachmanides was the clear victor of the debate, he had to flee Spain because of the resulting persecution. He moved to Israel and helped reestablish communal life in Jerusalem. He authored a classic commentary on the Pentateuch and a commentary on the Talmud.

Nachmanides, Pirush HaRamban, Bereishit 34:13

ורבים ישאלו: איך עשו בני יעקב הצדיקים המעשה הזה לשפוך דם נקי?

any will ask: How did Jacob's righteous sons commit this act, to spill innocent blood?

An Old Trend

TEXT 3

Bereishit (Genesis) 18:23, 25

וַיִּגַּשׁ אַבְרָהָם וַיֹּאמַר הַאַף תִּסְפֶּה צַדִּיק עִם רָשָׁע:...
חָלִלָה לְּךָ מֵעֲשֹׂת כַּדָּבָר הַזֶּה לְהָמִית צַדִּיק עִם רָשָׁע וְהָיָה כַצַּדִּיק כָּרָשָׁע
חָלִלָה לָּךְ הֲשֹׁפֵט כָּל הָאָרֶץ לֹא יַעֲשֶׂה מִשְׁפָּט:

nd Abraham approached and said, "Will You even destroy the righteous with the wicked?...

"Far be it from You to do a thing such as this, to put to death the righteous with the wicked so that the righteous should be like the wicked. Far be it from You! Will the Judge of the entire earth not perform justice?"

TEXT 4A

Bereishit (Genesis) 15:1

אַחַר הַדְּבָרִים הָאֵלֶּה הָיָה דְבַר ה' אֶל אַבְרָם בַּמַּחֲזֶה לֵאמֹר אַל תִּירָא אַבְרָם אָנֹכִי מָגֵן לָךְ שְׂכָרְךָ הַרְבֵּה מְאֹד:

After these incidents, the word of the Lord came to Abram in a vision, saying, "Fear not, Abram; I am your Shield; your reward is exceedingly great."

TEXT 4B

Midrash Bereishit Rabah, 44:4

היה אבינו אברהם מתפחד ואומר תאמר אותן אוכלסין שהרגתי שהיה בהם צדיק אחד וירא שמים אחד.

Abraham feared that among the peoples he had killed was a righteous tzadik or one who feared Heaven.

Bereishit Rabah
An early rabbinic commentary on the Book of Genesis. This Midrash bears the name of Rabbi Oshiya Rabah (Rabbi Oshiya "the Great") whose teaching opens this work. This Midrash provides textual exegeses and stories, expounds upon the biblical narrative, and develops and illustrates moral principles. Produced by the sages of the Talmud in the Land of Israel, its use of Aramaic closely resembles that of the Jerusalem Talmud. It was first printed in Constantinople in 1512 together with four other Midrashic works on the other four books of the Pentateuch.

TEXT 5A

Bereishit (Genesis) 32:8

וַיִּירָא יַעֲקֹב מְאֹד וַיֵּצֶר לוֹ וַיַּחַץ אֶת הָעָם אֲשֶׁר אִתּוֹ וְאֶת הַצֹּאן וְאֶת הַבָּקָר וְהַגְּמַלִּים לִשְׁנֵי מַחֲנוֹת:

Jacob became very frightened and was distressed; so he divided the people who were with him and the flocks and the cattle and the camels into two camps.

TEXT 5B

Rashi, loc. ad loc.

Rabbi Shlomo Yitzchaki (Rashi)
1040–1105
Most noted biblical and Talmudic commentator. Born in Troyes, France, Rashi studied in the famed *yeshivot* of Mainz and Worms. His commentaries on the Pentateuch and the Talmud, which focus on the straightforward meaning of the text, appear in virtually every edition of the Talmud and Bible.

"וַיִּירָא וַיֵּצֶר". וייְרא שמא יהרג, ויצר לו אם יהרוג הוא את אחרים.

Jacob became . . . frightened, and . . . distressed." He was frightened lest he be killed, and he was distressed that he might kill others.

Jacob's Culpability

A Broken Promise

TEXT 6A

Bereishit (Genesis) 35:1

וַיֹּאמֶר אֱלֹקִים אֶל יַעֲקֹב קוּם עֲלֵה בֵית אֵל וְשֶׁב שָׁם וַעֲשֵׂה שָׁם מִזְבֵּחַ
לָאֵ-ל הַנִּרְאֶה אֵלֶיךָ בְּבָרְחֲךָ מִפְּנֵי עֵשָׂו אָחִיךָ:

And G-d said to Jacob, "Arise and go up to Beth-el and reside there, and make there an altar to the G-d Who appeared to you when you fled from your brother Esau."

TEXT 6B

Midrash Tanchuma, Vayishlach, ch. 8

אמר לו הקדוש ברוך הוא: לא הגיעוך הצרות האלו, אלא על שאחרת
את נדרך, אם את מבקש שלא יגיעוך עוד צרה, קום עלה אל בית אל ועשה
שם מזבח לאותו מקום שנדרת לי שם נדר, אנכי הא-ל בית אל אשר
משחת שם מצבה, אשר נדרת לי שם נדר ... אמר הקדוש ברוך הוא
ליעקב: בשעת עקתא נדרא בשעת רווחא שמטי? כשהיית בצרה נדרת,
וכשאתה בריוח שכחת?!

The Holy One, blessed be He, said to him, "These troubles only came upon you because you delayed [the fulfillment of] your vow. If

Midrash Tanchuma

A midrashic work bearing the name of Rabbi Tanchuma, a 4th-century Talmudic sage quoted often in this work. Midrash is the designation of a particular genre of rabbinic literature usually forming a running commentary on specific books of the Bible. *Midrash Tanchuma* provides textual exegeses, expounds upon the biblical narrative, and develops and illustrates moral principles. *Tanchuma* is unique in that many of its sections commence with a halachic discussion, which subsequently leads into non-halachic teachings.

you seek to avoid further distress, 'Arise and go up to Beth-el and abide there, and make an altar' at that place you originally made your vow to me,' I am the G-d of Beth-el, where you anointed a monument [after stopping there on the way to Charan years earlier], where you vowed a vow..."

Said the Holy One, blessed be He, to Yaakov: At a time of distress, you dedicate; at a time of favor, you forget? When you were in trouble, you vowed, and once you were comfortable, you forgot?!

TEXT 7A

Bereishit (Genesis) 33:17–19

וַיַּעֲקֹב נָסַע סֻכֹּתָה וַיִּבֶן לוֹ בָּיִת וּלְמִקְנֵהוּ עָשָׂה סֻכֹּת עַל כֵּן קָרָא שֵׁם הַמָּקוֹם סֻכּוֹת:

וַיָּבֹא יַעֲקֹב שָׁלֵם עִיר שְׁכֶם אֲשֶׁר בְּאֶרֶץ כְּנַעַן בְּבֹאוֹ מִפַּדַּן אֲרָם וַיִּחַן אֶת פְּנֵי הָעִיר:

וַיִּקֶן אֶת חֶלְקַת הַשָּׂדֶה אֲשֶׁר נָטָה שָׁם אָהֳלוֹ מִיַּד בְּנֵי חֲמוֹר אֲבִי שְׁכֶם בְּמֵאָה קְשִׂיטָה:

nd Jacob traveled to Succot and built himself a house, and for his cattle he made booths; therefore he named the place Succot.

And Jacob came safely [to] the city of Shechem, which is in the land of Canaan, when he came from Padan Aram, and he encamped before the city.

And he bought the part of the field where he had pitched his tent from the sons of Hamor, the father of Shechem, for a hundred kesitas.

TEXT 7B

Rashi, ad loc.

"ויבן לו בית". שהה שם שמונה עשר חדש, קיץ וחורף וקיץ. סכות קיץ,
בית חורף, סכות קיץ.

"And built himself a house." He stayed there eighteen months: summer, winter, and summer. "Succot" denotes summer. "A house" denotes winter, and [again] "succot" denotes summer.

It Takes a Village

Jacob's Reaction

TEXT 8A

Bereishit (Genesis) 34:30

וַיֹּאמֶר יַעֲקֹב אֶל שִׁמְעוֹן וְאֶל לֵוִי עֲכַרְתֶּם אֹתִי לְהַבְאִישֵׁנִי בְּיֹשֵׁב הָאָרֶץ בַּכְּנַעֲנִי וּבַפְּרִזִּי וַאֲנִי מְתֵי מִסְפָּר וְנֶאֶסְפוּ עָלַי וְהִכּוּנִי וְנִשְׁמַדְתִּי אֲנִי וּבֵיתִי:

Thereupon, Jacob said to Simeon and to Levi, "You have troubled me, to discredit me among the inhabitants of the land, among the Canaanites and among the Perizzites, and I am few in number, and they will gather against me, and I and my household will be destroyed."

TEXT 8B

Ibid., verse 31

וַיֹּאמְרוּ הַכְזוֹנָה יַעֲשֶׂה אֶת אֲחוֹתֵנוּ:

And they said, "Shall he make our sister like a harlot?"

On Jacob's Deathbed

TEXT 9A

Bereishit (Genesis) 49:5–7

שִׁמְעוֹן וְלֵוִי אַחִים כְּלֵי חָמָס מְכֵרֹתֵיהֶם:

בְּסֹדָם אַל תָּבֹא נַפְשִׁי בִּקְהָלָם אַל תֵּחַד כְּבֹדִי כִּי בְאַפָּם הָרְגוּ אִישׁ וּבִרְצֹנָם עִקְּרוּ שׁוֹר:

אָרוּר אַפָּם כִּי עָז וְעֶבְרָתָם כִּי קָשָׁתָה אֲחַלְּקֵם בְּיַעֲקֹב וַאֲפִיצֵם בְּיִשְׂרָאֵל:

Simeon and Levi are brothers; violent (chamas, alt.: stolen) instruments are their weapons.

Let my soul not enter their counsel; my honor, you shall not join their assembly, for in their wrath they killed a man, and with their will they hamstrung a bull.

Cursed be their wrath for it is mighty, and their anger because it is harsh. I will separate them throughout Jacob, and I will scatter them throughout Israel.

TEXT 9B

Rashi, ad loc.

"כלי חמס". אומנות זו של רציחה, חמס הוא בידיהם, מברכת עשו היא,
זו אומנות שלו היא, ואתם חמסתם אותה הימנו.
..."כי באפם הרגו איש". אלו חמור ואנשי שכם.

"Stolen instruments." This craft of murder is in their hands wrongfully, [for] it is [part] of Esau's blessing. It is his craft, and you (Simeon and Levi) have stolen it from him.

..."For in their wrath they killed a man." These are Hamor and the men of Shechem.

Question: Flip Flop?

TEXT 10

Nachmanides, Pirush Haramban, Bereishit 34:13

ויעקב אמר להם בכאן [רק] כי הביאוהו בסכנה שנאמר "עכרתם אותי
להבאישני", ושם ארר אפם כי עשו חמס לאנשי העיר.

Here, Jacob only told them that they had endangered him, as it says, "You troubled me, to discredit me." There he cursed their wrath because they committed injustice against the people of the city.

Judicial Dereliction

TEXT 11A

Babylonian Talmud, Sanhedrin 57a

אזהרה שלהן—זו היא מיתתן.

Their prohibition [of one of the Noahide laws] carries within it the death penalty.

Babylonian Talmud
A literary work of monumental proportions that draws upon the legal, spiritual, intellectual, ethical, and historical traditions of Judaism. The 37 tractates of the Babylonian Talmud contain the teachings of the Jewish sages from the period after the destruction of the 2nd Temple through the 5th century CE. It has served as the primary vehicle for the transmission of the Oral Law and the education of Jews over the centuries; it is the entry point for all subsequent legal, ethical, and theological Jewish scholarship.

TEXT 11B

Maimonides, Mishneh Torah, Laws of Kings 9:14

וכיצד מצווין הן על הדינין?
חייבין להושיב דיינין ושופטים בכל פלך ופלך לדון בשש מצות אלו ולהזהיר את העם. ובן נח שעבר על אחת משבע מצות אלו יהרג בסייף. ומפני זה נתחייבו כל בעלי שכם הריגה, שהרי שכם גזל והם ראו וידעו ולא דנוהו.

How must the gentiles fulfill the commandment to establish laws and courts? They are obligated to set up judges and magistrates in every major city to render judgment concerning these six mitzvot and to admonish the people regarding their observance.

A gentile who transgresses one of these seven commands shall be executed by decapitation. For this

Rabbi Moshe ben Maimon
(Maimonides, Rambam)
1135–1204
Halachist, philosopher, author, and physician. Maimonides was born in Cordoba, Spain. After the conquest of Cordoba by the Almohads, he fled Spain and eventually settled in Cairo, Egypt. There, he became the leader of the Jewish community and served as court physician to the vizier of Egypt. He is most noted for authoring the *Mishneh Torah*, an encyclopedic arrangement of Jewish law, and for his philosophical work, *Guide for the Perplexed*. His rulings on Jewish law are integral to the formation of halachic consensus.

reason, all the inhabitants of Shechem were liable for the death sentence. Shechem kidnapped; they observed and were aware of his deeds, but did not judge him.

Revisiting Jacob's Critique

TEXT 12

Chaim ibn Attar, Or Hachayim, Bereishit 34:31

צריך לדעת מה תשובה זו עושה למיחוש יעקב על השמדתו הוא וביתו... אדרבא יסתכנו בין האומות כשיראו שבזוי אחד שלט בבת יעקב ופעל ועשה כחפצו ורצונו לא תהיה לשונאיהם תקומה בין העמים, ואדרבה בזה תהיה חתתם על העמים וירעדו מפניהם.

Rabbi Chayim ibn Atar
(Or Hachayim)
1696–1743
Biblical exegete, kabbalist, and Talmudist. Rabbi Atar, born in Meknes, Morocco, was a prominent member of the Moroccan rabbinate and later immigrated to the Land of Israel. He is most famous for his *Or Hachayim*, a popular commentary on the Torah. The famed Jewish historian and bibliophile Rabbi Chaim Yosef David Azulai was among his most notable disciples.

One must understand, what did this answer do for Jacob's fears that he and his family would be annihilated?...

[Simeon and Levi's answer was that] on the contrary, [if they had not responded], they would be endangering themselves amongst the local peoples; once they all see how some lowlife seized Jacob's daughter and did whatever he wanted, they would have no standing amongst the nations of the region. On the contrary, [as a result of their actions] their dread fell upon the nations so that they trembled before them.

Sodom 2.0

TEXT 13A

Nachmanides, op. cit.

ואין הדברים הללו נכונים בעיני, שאם כן היה יעקב אבינו חייב להיות
קודם וזוכה במיתתם. ואם פחד מהם, למה כעס על בניו וארר אפם
אחר כמה זמנים [בפרשת ויחי] וענש אותם וחלקם והפיצם, והלא הם
זכו ועשו מצוה ובטחו באלוקים והצילם?

In my eyes, [Maimonides'] words do not seem correct. If so, our father Jacob would have been obligated to take part in their capital punishment himself. And if he [abstained because he] was afraid, why was he angry with his sons? [Why did he] curse their anger later on, and punish them with "separate them" and "scatter them"? Hadn't they done a mitzvah, trusted in G-d, and were saved by Him?

TEXT 13B

Ibid.

מכלל המצוה הזו שיושיבו דיינים בכל עיר ועיר כישראל ואם לא עשו
כן אינם נהרגים, שזו מצות עשה בהם ולא אמרו אלא אזהרה שלהם זו
היא מיתתן ולא תיקרא אזהרה אלא המניעה בלאו.

Implied in this mitzvah is the duty to set up judges in every city, just as the Jews [are obligated to do]. But if they do not so, they are not killed, since this is a positive commandment. It was only ever said that "their prohibitions are capital offenses," and only abstaining to fulfill a negative commandment can be considered a "prohibition" (azhara).

TEXT 13C

Ibid.

אנשי שכם וכל שבעה עממים, עובדי עבודה זרה ומגלי עריות ועושים
כל תועבות השם וכך צווח הכתוב בכמה מקומות... "את כל התועבות
האל עשו"... אלא שאין הדבר מסור ליעקב ובניו לעשות בהם הדין.
אבל ענין שכם, כי בני יעקב בעבור שהיו אנשי שכם רשעים ודמם
חשוב להם כמים רצו שמעון ולוי להינקם בהם בחרב נוקמת.

The people of Shechem, along with all of the seven nations [inhabiting the Land of Canaan at that time], engaged in idol-worship, sexual immorality, and every other abomination. Thus, the

Torah decried their conduct in numerous places ... for "all of these abominations they committed."...

It was not entrusted to the sons of Jacob to bring them to justice, but the sons of Yaakov considered the blood of the people of Shechem like water, since they were wicked [and thus their lives were already forfeited], and therefore Simeon and Levi wanted to avenge them with a vengeful sword.

TEXT 13D

Ibid.

ויעקב אמר להם בכאן [בפרשתנו] כי הביאוהו בסכנה... ושם ארר אפם... והרגו אותם חנם כי לא הרעו להם כלל.

Jacob said to them over here that they had put him in danger ... and over there "may their anger be cursed" for ... killing them without cause, since they had not wronged them personally at all.

What Drives You?

A Sigh and an Answer

Once, when the Rebbe Rashab was a young child, he and his brother, Rabbi Zalman Aharon ("Raza"), who was a year older, were playing "Rebbe and Chasid." Zalman Aharon, playing the role of "Rebbe," sat on a chair and straightened his hat, and the young Rashab belted himself with a prayer sash, just as a Chasid does in preparation for his audience with a Rebbe. The Rebbe Rashab told his brother, the "Rebbe," about a spiritual difficulty he was facing, and asked him how to correct it.

His brother duly prescribed for him a course of action.

Their mother, Rebbetzin Rivkah, had observed her children playing, and she noticed that the Rebbe Rashab did not follow his brother's advice.

When she queried him about this, he replied, "My brother is not a Rebbe. When a person comes to a Rebbe with a spiritual difficulty, a true Rebbe first gives up an understanding sigh and only then offers advice. My brother didn't sigh; he just answered."

Ulterior Motive

TEXT 14

The Lubavitcher Rebbe, Likutei Sichot, vol. 5, p. 161, fn. 71

כאשר ענו ליעקב "הכזונה וגו'" ,קיבל את המענה. אלא שמכל מקום הוכיח אותם לאחר זמן על זה, כי לאחר שראה ש"באפם הרגו איש",

ושוב "ברצונם עקרו שור"—היה אצלו הוכחה שיש אצלם נטייה לזה (גם) מצד טבעם, וגם במעשה שכם היתה תערובת מטבע זה שלהם.

When Simeon and Levi initially responded to Jacob, "Shall he make our sister like a harlot?" he accepted their response. Nevertheless, he rebuked them for their actions later on because once he saw that "they killed a man in their wrath," and then "hamstrung a bull," it was proven to him that they have a natural tendency [for violence], and that this tendency contributed to their actions in Shechem.

Rabbi Menachem Mendel Schneerson
1902–1994
The towering Jewish leader of the 20th century, known as "the Lubavitcher Rebbe," or simply as "the Rebbe." Born in southern Ukraine, the Rebbe escaped Nazi-occupied Europe, arriving in the U.S. in June 1941. The Rebbe inspired and guided the revival of traditional Judaism after the European devastation, impacting virtually every Jewish community the world over. The Rebbe often emphasized that the performance of just one additional good deed could usher in the era of Moshiach. The Rebbe's scholarly talks and writings have been printed in more than 200 volumes.

How to Eat Nonkosher

In 1825, Czar Nicholas I, a cruel man, his religious convictions inflamed by the Russian Church's antisemitism, ascended to the Russian throne. Determined to tear the Jewish people from their faith, he expanded the draft to conscript Jewish boys into 25 years of military service, beginning with the notorious "Canton" schools. From a tender young age, these boys underwent a thoroughly Christian military education and service after, of course, undergoing a forced baptism and conversion.

Once, a group of these "Cantonists" managed to visit the third Lubavitcher Rebbe, the Tzemach Tzedek, and described to him their difficult lives. They were deprived of any link to their Jewish heritage, forced to attend church, and made to eat nonkosher food. On this final point, they were unsure of what to do. Perhaps, they asked, it would be better to fast, at risk to their lives, rather than eat *treif* meat.

The Rebbe understood well their dilemma their profound spiritual anguish. The brutal demands of military service meant that they had to take whatever food they could get. But to eat *treif*?

"Eat," he told them, "but make sure not to lick your fingers!"

Cruel Intentions

TEXT 15

Nachmanides, Pirush Haramban, Shemot 7:3

השאלה אשר ישאלו הכל: אם ה' הקשה את לבו—מה פשעו?

he question that everyone asks: If G-d hardened his heart—what was his crime?

TEXT 16

The Lubavitcher Rebbe, Likutei Sichot, vol. 31, p. 31

...זה ש"מאן לשלח העם" לא היה (רק) מפני שהקדוש ברוך הוא חיזק את לבו, אלא ש(גם) הוא מצד עצמו הכביד את לבו שלא לשלח את בני ישראל, ולכן ראוי הוא להענש על זה.

[ועל דרך התירוץ בספרים על הקושיא—איך העניש הקדוש ברוך הוא המצריים על שהעבידו את בני ישראל בפרך, והרי הקדוש ברוך הוא גזר

עליהם "ועבדום וענו אותם"? דזה שהמצריים העבידו כו' ועינו את בני ישראל לא היה כדי לקיים גזירת הקדוש ברוך הוא, אלא מפני רשעות לבם, ולכן נענשו על כך.]

Pharaoh's refusal to let the Jewish people go was not (only) because G-d had hardened his heart, but (also) because he had strengthened his own resolve not to send off the Jewish people; therefore, he was deserving of punishment.

[This is similar to the answer proposed for the question of why G-d punished the Egyptians for enslaving the Jews if He Himself had decreed that "they will enslave and oppress them": the Egyptians hadn't been enslaving and oppressing the Jewish people in order to fulfill G-d's decree, but out of their own wickedness. Therefore they were punished for it.]

The Thought Counts

Story. Friends Stay Friends

Zalman Schachter (Shalomi) was for decades a well-known figure within American Jewry, until his passing in 2014. Originally he had been a Chabad Chasid. After being ordained as a rabbi, he spent some time teaching Judaism on campuses throughout North America, but eventually he drifted away from halachic observance. Schachter broke from Chabad Chasidus and went on to co-found the Jewish Renewal movement.

His departure came as a painful blow for the Chasidim who knew him, and made him profoundly estranged from Chabad circles.

At some point, the Rebbe asked Rabbi Avrohom Shem-Tov, who had spent time in the *yeshivah* along with Schachter, whether he was still on friendly terms with his former peer. Rabbi Shem-Tov answered in the affirmative.

"Do you know if he has a *parnasah*?" asked the Rebbe. Does he have some sort of livelihood; is he capable of supporting himself? Rabbi Shem-Tov reponded that he wasn't familiar with that aspect of his friend's life.

"But how can you be his friend," said the Rebbe, "if you don't know how he's managing to support himself, and whether he might need some help from others?"

8

VAYESHEV

Do Something, Anything

The Key to Getting Unstuck

Dedicated in loving memory of Dr. Yehuda Landes

לע"נ יהודה בן מאיר ז"ל לאנדעס | נפטר כ"ב כסלו תשס"ה

PARASHA OVERVIEW
Vayeshev

Jacob settles in Hebron with his twelve sons. His favorite is seventeen-year-old Joseph, whose brothers are jealous of the preferential treatment he receives from his father, such as a precious many-colored coat that Jacob makes for Joseph. Joseph relates to his brothers two of his dreams which foretell that he is destined to rule over them, increasing their envy and hatred towards him.

Simeon and Levi plot to kill him, but Reuben suggests that they throw him into a pit instead, intending to come back later and save him. While Joseph is in the pit, Judah has him sold to a band of passing Ishmaelites. The brothers dip Joseph's special coat in the blood of a goat and show it to their father, leading him to believe that his most beloved son was devoured by a wild beast.

Judah marries and has three children. The eldest, Er, dies young and childless, and his wife, Tamar, is given in levirate marriage to the second son, Onan. Onan sins by spilling his seed, and he too meets an early death. Judah is reluctant to have his third son marry her. Determined to have a child from Judah's family,

Tamar disguises herself as a prostitute and seduces Judah himself. Judah hears that his daughter-in-law has become pregnant and orders her executed for harlotry, but when Tamar produces some personal effects he left with her as a pledge for payment, he publicly admits that he is the father. Tamar gives birth to twin sons, Peretz (an ancestor of King David) and Zerach.

Joseph is taken to Egypt and sold to Potiphar, the minister in charge of Pharaoh's slaughterhouses. G-d blesses everything he does, and soon he is made overseer of all his master's property. Potiphar's wife desires the handsome and charismatic lad; when Joseph rejects her advances, she tells her husband that the Hebrew slave tried to force himself on her, and has him thrown into prison. Joseph gains the trust and admiration of his jailers, who appoint him to a position of authority in the prison administration.

In prison, Joseph meets Pharaoh's chief butler and chief baker, both incarcerated for offending their royal master. Both have disturbing dreams, which Joseph interprets; in three days, he tells them, the butler will be released and the baker hanged. Joseph asks the butler to intercede on his behalf with Pharaoh. Joseph's predictions are fulfilled, but the butler forgets all about Joseph and does nothing for him.

A Tale of Two Dreams

Joseph the Interpreter

TEXT 1

Bereishit (Genesis) ch. 40

וַיְהִי אַחַר הַדְּבָרִים הָאֵלֶּה חָטְאוּ מַשְׁקֵה מֶלֶךְ מִצְרַיִם וְהָאֹפֶה לַאֲדֹנֵיהֶם לְמֶלֶךְ מִצְרָיִם:

וַיִּקְצֹף פַּרְעֹה עַל שְׁנֵי סָרִיסָיו עַל שַׂר הַמַּשְׁקִים וְעַל שַׂר הָאוֹפִים:

וַיִּתֵּן אֹתָם בְּמִשְׁמַר בֵּית שַׂר הַטַּבָּחִים אֶל בֵּית הַסֹּהַר מְקוֹם אֲשֶׁר יוֹסֵף אָסוּר שָׁם:

וַיִּפְקֹד שַׂר הַטַּבָּחִים אֶת יוֹסֵף אִתָּם וַיְשָׁרֶת אֹתָם וַיִּהְיוּ יָמִים בְּמִשְׁמָר:

וַיַּחַלְמוּ חֲלוֹם שְׁנֵיהֶם אִישׁ חֲלֹמוֹ בְּלַיְלָה אֶחָד אִישׁ כְּפִתְרוֹן חֲלֹמוֹ הַמַּשְׁקֶה וְהָאֹפֶה אֲשֶׁר לְמֶלֶךְ מִצְרַיִם אֲשֶׁר אֲסוּרִים בְּבֵית הַסֹּהַר:

וַיָּבֹא אֲלֵיהֶם יוֹסֵף בַּבֹּקֶר וַיַּרְא אֹתָם וְהִנָּם זֹעֲפִים:

וַיִּשְׁאַל אֶת סְרִיסֵי פַרְעֹה אֲשֶׁר אִתּוֹ בְמִשְׁמַר בֵּית אֲדֹנָיו לֵאמֹר מַדּוּעַ פְּנֵיכֶם רָעִים הַיּוֹם:

וַיֹּאמְרוּ אֵלָיו חֲלוֹם חָלַמְנוּ וּפֹתֵר אֵין אֹתוֹ וַיֹּאמֶר אֲלֵהֶם יוֹסֵף הֲלוֹא לֵאלֹקִים פִּתְרֹנִים סַפְּרוּ נָא לִי:

וַיְסַפֵּר שַׂר הַמַּשְׁקִים אֶת חֲלֹמוֹ לְיוֹסֵף וַיֹּאמֶר לוֹ בַּחֲלוֹמִי וְהִנֵּה גֶפֶן לְפָנָי:

וּבַגֶּפֶן שְׁלֹשָׁה שָׂרִיגִם וְהִיא כְפֹרַחַת עָלְתָה נִצָּהּ הִבְשִׁילוּ אַשְׁכְּלֹתֶיהָ עֲנָבִים:

וְכוֹס פַּרְעֹה בְּיָדִי וָאֶקַּח אֶת הָעֲנָבִים וָאֶשְׂחַט אֹתָם אֶל כּוֹס פַּרְעֹה וָאֶתֵּן אֶת הַכּוֹס עַל כַּף פַּרְעֹה:

וַיֹּאמֶר לוֹ יוֹסֵף זֶה פִּתְרֹנוֹ שְׁלֹשֶׁת הַשָּׂרִגִים שְׁלֹשֶׁת יָמִים הֵם:

בְּעוֹד שְׁלֹשֶׁת יָמִים יִשָּׂא פַרְעֹה אֶת רֹאשֶׁךָ וַהֲשִׁיבְךָ עַל כַּנֶּךָ וְנָתַתָּ כוֹס פַּרְעֹה בְּיָדוֹ כַּמִּשְׁפָּט הָרִאשׁוֹן אֲשֶׁר הָיִיתָ מַשְׁקֵהוּ:

כִּי אִם זְכַרְתַּנִי אִתְּךָ כַּאֲשֶׁר יִיטַב לָךְ וְעָשִׂיתָ נָּא עִמָּדִי חָסֶד וְהִזְכַּרְתַּנִי אֶל פַּרְעֹה וְהוֹצֵאתַנִי מִן הַבַּיִת הַזֶּה:

כִּי גֻנֹּב גֻּנַּבְתִּי מֵאֶרֶץ הָעִבְרִים וְגַם פֹּה לֹא עָשִׂיתִי מְאוּמָה כִּי שָׂמוּ אֹתִי בַּבּוֹר:

וַיַּרְא שַׂר הָאֹפִים כִּי טוֹב פָּתָר וַיֹּאמֶר אֶל יוֹסֵף אַף אֲנִי בַּחֲלוֹמִי וְהִנֵּה שְׁלֹשָׁה סַלֵּי חֹרִי עַל רֹאשִׁי:

וּבַסַּל הָעֶלְיוֹן מִכֹּל מַאֲכַל פַּרְעֹה מַעֲשֵׂה אֹפֶה וְהָעוֹף אֹכֵל אֹתָם מִן הַסַּל מֵעַל רֹאשִׁי:

וַיַּעַן יוֹסֵף וַיֹּאמֶר זֶה פִּתְרֹנוֹ שְׁלֹשֶׁת הַסַּלִּים שְׁלֹשֶׁת יָמִים הֵם:

בְּעוֹד שְׁלֹשֶׁת יָמִים יִשָּׂא פַרְעֹה אֶת רֹאשְׁךָ מֵעָלֶיךָ וְתָלָה אוֹתְךָ עַל עֵץ וְאָכַל הָעוֹף אֶת בְּשָׂרְךָ מֵעָלֶיךָ:

וַיְהִי בַּיּוֹם הַשְּׁלִישִׁי יוֹם הֻלֶּדֶת אֶת פַּרְעֹה וַיַּעַשׂ מִשְׁתֶּה לְכָל עֲבָדָיו וַיִּשָּׂא אֶת רֹאשׁ שַׂר הַמַּשְׁקִים וְאֶת רֹאשׁ שַׂר הָאֹפִים בְּתוֹךְ עֲבָדָיו:

וַיָּשֶׁב אֶת שַׂר הַמַּשְׁקִים עַל מַשְׁקֵהוּ וַיִּתֵּן הַכּוֹס עַל כַּף פַּרְעֹה:

וְאֵת שַׂר הָאֹפִים תָּלָה כַּאֲשֶׁר פָּתַר לָהֶם יוֹסֵף:

וְלֹא זָכַר שַׂר הַמַּשְׁקִים אֶת יוֹסֵף וַיִּשְׁכָּחֵהוּ:

ow, it came about after these events that the cupbearer of the king of Egypt and the baker sinned against their master, against the king of Egypt.

And Pharaoh became incensed at his two chamberlains, at the chief cupbearer and at the chief baker.

And he placed them in the prison of the house of the chief of the slaughterers, into the prison, the place where Joseph was imprisoned.

And the chief of the slaughterers appointed Joseph [to be] with them, and he served them, and they were a year in prison.

Now, both of them dreamed a dream, each one his dream on the same night, each man according to the interpretation of his dream, the cupbearer and the baker of the king of Egypt, who were confined in the prison.

And Joseph came to them in the morning, and he saw them and, behold, they were troubled.

And he asked Pharaoh's chamberlains who were with him in the prison of his master's house, saying, "Why are your faces sad today?"

And they said to him, "We have dreamed a dream, and there is no interpreter for it." Joseph said to them, "Don't interpretations belong to G-d? Tell [them] to me now."

So the chief cupbearer related his dream to Joseph, and he said to him, "In my dream, behold, a vine is before me.

"And on the vine are three tendrils, and it seemed to be blossoming, and its buds came out; [then] its clusters ripened into grapes.

"And Pharaoh's cup was in my hand, and I took the grapes and squeezed them into Pharaoh's cup, and I placed the cup on Pharaoh's palm."

And Joseph said to him, "This is its meaning: the three tendrils are three days.

"In another three days, Pharaoh will number you [with the other officers], and he will restore you to your position, and you will place Pharaoh's cup into his hand, according to [your] previous custom, when you were his cupbearer.

"But, remember me when things go well with you, and please do me a favor and mention me to Pharaoh, and you will get me out of this house.

"For I was stolen from the land of the Hebrews, and here, too, I have done nothing for which they have put me into the dungeon."

Now, the chief baker saw that he had interpreted well. So he said to Joseph, "Me too! In my dream, behold, there were three wicker baskets on my head.

"And in the topmost basket were all kinds of Pharaoh's food, the work of a baker, and the birds were eating them from the basket atop my head."

And Joseph replied and said, "This is its meaning: the three baskets represent three days.

"In another three days, Pharaoh will remove your head from you and hang you on a gallows, and the birds will eat your flesh off you."

Now, it came about on the third day, Pharaoh's birthday, that Pharaoh made a feast for all his servants, *and he counted the chief cupbearer and chief baker among his servants.*

And he restored the chief cupbearer to his [position as] cupbearer, and he placed the cup on Pharaoh's palm.

And the chief baker he hanged, as Joseph had interpreted to them.

But the chief cupbearer did not remember Joseph, and he forgot him.

Watch What You Say

TEXT 2

Talmud Tractate Berachot, 55b

שמואל כי הוה חזי חלמא בישא אמר "וחלומות השוא ידברו". כי הוה חזי חלמא טבא אמר וכי החלומות השוא ידברו, והכתיב "בחלום אדבר בו..."

אמר רבי ביזנא בר זבדא אמר רבי עקיבא אמר רבי פנדא אמר רבי נחום אמר רבי בירים משום זקן אחד ומנו רבי בנאה: עשרים וארבעה פותרי חלומות היו בירושלים. פעם אחת חלמתי חלום והלכתי אצל כולם ומה שפתר לי זה לא פתר לי זה, וכולם נתקיימו בי לקיים מה שנאמר "כל החלומות הולכים אחר הפה".

אטו כל החלומות הולכים אחר הפה?... דאמר רבי אלעזר: מנין שכל החלומות הולכין אחר הפה, שנאמר "ויהי כאשר פתר לנו כן היה".

אמר רבא והוא דמפשר ליה מעין חלמיה שנאמר "איש כחלומו פתר".

When Shmuel would have a bad dream, he would say [citing the verse,] "Dreams speak falsely." When he would have a good dream, he would ask this as a rhetorical question, "Dreams speak falsely? But the verse states, 'I will speak to him in a dream…'"

Rabbi Bizna bar Zavda said in the name of Rabbi Akiva, who said in the name of Rabbi Pando who said in the name of Rabbi Nachum who said in the name of Birim who said in the name of a certain elder—Rabbi Bana'ah: There were twenty-four dream interpreters in Jerusalem. I once had a dream and went to see all of them. Each one gave me a different interpretation, and every interpretation was fulfilled. This fulfills what is said that "all dreams follow the interpretation"…

For Rabbi Elazar said, "How do we know that all dreams follow their interpretation? The verse states, 'And it came to pass just as he had interpreted for us.'"

Rava said, "This applies only when the interpretation matches the dream, as it says, 'he interpreted according to his dream.'"

Babylonian Talmud
A literary work of monumental proportions that draws upon the legal, spiritual, intellectual, ethical, and historical traditions of Judaism. The 37 tractates of the Babylonian Talmud contain the teachings of the Jewish sages from the period after the destruction of the 2nd Temple through the 5th century CE. It has served as the primary vehicle for the transmission of the Oral Law and the education of Jews over the centuries; it is the entry point for all subsequent legal, ethical, and theological Jewish scholarship.

Divine Inspiration

TEXT 3

Rabbi Don Yitzchak Abarbanel
1437–1508
Biblical exegete and
statesman. Abarbanel was
born in Lisbon, Portugal
and served as a minister in
the court of King Alfonso V
of Portugal. After intrigues
at court led to accusations
against him, he fled to Spain,
where he once again served
as a counselor to royalty. It
is claimed that Abarbanel
offered King Ferdinand and
Queen Isabella large sums
of money for the revocation
of their Edict of Expulsion of
1492, but to no avail. After
the expulsion, he eventually
settled in Italy where he wrote
a commentary on Scripture, as
well as other venerated works.

Rabbi Don Yitzchak Abarbanel, Pirush Abarbanel, ad loc.

ויוסף השיבם: "הלא לאלקים פתרונים". רוצה לומר, טעות היא בידכם
לחשוב שישלם פתרון החלומות במלאכה וחכמה. ואין הדבר כן, כי
יוכל משל אחד לרמוז על נמשלים רבים. ולכן רחוק הוא שהפותר
יפתור אמת תמיד ומבלי עירוב דברים כוזבים. דעו כי "הלא לאלקים
פתרונים", רוצה לומר לא יוכל אדם לפתור חלומות בשלמות, אם לא
בהיות רוח אלהים נוססה בו. כי בכוח רוח הקודש יגיד הנעלם.

Joseph replied, "Don't interpretations belong
to G-d?" In other words, don't think that your
dreams can be fully interpreted with human effort and wisdom, for one detail of a dream can allude to
many different interpretations. Therefore, it is almost
impossible to interpret dreams without mixing some
false details into the interpretation, for "interpretations
belong to G-d," i.e., it is only possible to fully interpret
a dream by Divine Inspiration, that can reveal what
is hidden.

TEXT 4A

Rabbi Shlomo Yitzchaki (Rashi)
1040–1105
Most noted biblical and Talmudic commentator. Born in Troyes, France, Rashi studied in the famed *yeshivot* of Mainz and Worms. His commentaries on the Pentateuch and the Talmud, which focus on the straightforward meaning of the text, appear in virtually every edition of the Talmud and Bible.

Rashi to v. 5

"אִישׁ כְּפִתְרוֹן חֲלֹמוֹ." כָּל אֶחָד חָלַם חֲלוֹם הַדּוֹמֶה לְפִתְרוֹן הֶעָתִיד לָבֹא עֲלֵיהֶם.

"Each man according to the interpretation of his dream." Each one dreamed a dream similar to the interpretation destined to befall them.

TEXT 4B

Rabbi Dovid Halevi Segal (*Taz*)
1586–1667
Talmudist and halachist. Rabbi Segal is widely known as *Taz*, the initials of his magnum opus, *Turei Zahav*, an important commentary on the Shulchan Aruch. Rabbi Segal served as the rabbi in the city of Ostrog, Poland, but was forced to flee due to the Chmielnicki Massacre of 1648–1649. He later served as the rabbi of Lvov.

Rabbi Dovid Halevi Segal, Turei Zahav ad loc.

שֶׁלֹּא תֹּאמַר שֶׁמִּצַּד שֵׂכְלוֹ פָּתַר הַחֲלוֹמוֹת דְּהַיְנוּ לְפִי שֶׁכָּל בְּנֵי אָדָם שֶׁפּוֹתְרִין לְפִי הֶקֵּשׁ הָעִנְיָן לְפִי הַחֲלוֹם, דְּזֶה אֵינוֹ, אֶלָּא הַחֲלוֹם הָיָה מוֹרֶה עַל הַפִּתְרוֹן לֹא עַל הַפִּתְרוֹן שֶׁל יוֹסֵף...וּבֶאֱמֶת מֻכְרָח זֶה, דִּלְפִי שֶׂכֶל הָאֱנוֹשִׁי הָיָה לוֹ לְיוֹס, לִפְתּוֹר גַּם חֲלוֹם שַׂר הָאוֹפִים לְטוֹב, וְלוֹמַר דָּמָה שֶׁחָלַם שֶׁהָעוֹף אוֹכֵל מֵהַסַּל הַיְנוּ מֵהַסַּל הָיְנוּ פַּרְעֹה... וְגַם כָּאן הָיְתָה הַסְּבָרָא לִפְתּוֹר גַּם כֵּן שֶׁפַּרְעֹה יֹאכַל מִן הַסַּל שֶׁעַל רֹאשׁוֹ כִּי דֶּרֶךְ הַסַּל לָשֵׂאת עַל הָרֹאשׁ, וְאִם כֵּן לָמָּה פָּתַר לוֹ יוֹסֵף לְרָעָה, אֶלָּא וַדַּאי כִּי רוּחַ ה' הָיָה בּוֹ וְיוֹדֵעַ מַה שֶׁנִּגְזַר עָלָיו בֶּאֱמֶת.

Joseph did not interpret the dreams according to his human understanding, by focusing on what the details in the dream represented. Rather, the dreams reflected interpretations different from what Joseph would have given using basic human understanding…

Using human dream-interpretation capability, Joseph would have interpreted the baker's dream positively as well, explaining that the birds eating from the basket represent Pharaoh eating the baker's bread once more... Similarly, he would have interpreted that Pharaoh would once more eat from the basket upon the baker's head, for it was common to carry baskets on the head. So, why did Joseph give such a dire interpretation?

Certainly it is because the Divine Spirit was within him and he knew what was truly decreed for them...

The Importance of Faith

TEXT 5

Rabbi Tuviah Liskin, Kerem Tuviah ad loc.

ונראה לומר שבהנהגת שר האופים היה חסרון. והוא שכאשר אמר
להם יוסף "הלא לאלוקים פתרונים", מיד הציע בפניו שר המשקים את
החלים, כי האמין לדברים, ואילו שר האופים חיכה, ורק כאשר ראה "כי
טוב פתר" אז סיפר גם הוא את החלום. בשל הנהגה זו שהיה בו חסרון
באמונה לא עלה פתרונו יפה, ואילו שר המשקים שמיהר לספר זכה
ופתרונו היה לטובה.

The baker's conduct was deficient: When Joseph told them that "interpretations belong to G-d," the butler immediately related his dream, for he was a believer. But the baker stalled; only after he saw that "Joseph had interpreted well" the butler's dream did he proceed to relate his own. In this he lacked faith, and therefore his interpretation did not turn out well, while the butler who didn't hesitate was meritorious and received a good interpretation.

Between Life and Death

The Butler's Four Cups

TEXT 6

Jerusalem Talmud
A commentary to the Mishnah, compiled during the 4th and 5th centuries. The Jerusalem Talmud predates its Babylonian counterpart by 100 years and is written in both Hebrew and Aramaic. While the Babylonian Talmud remains the most authoritative source for Jewish law, the Jerusalem Talmud remains an invaluable source for the spiritual, intellectual, ethical, historical, and legal traditions of Judaism.

Jerusalem Talmud, Tractate Pesachim 10:1

מניין לארבעה כוסות... רבי יהושע בן לוי אמר כנגד ארבעה כוסות
של פרעה.

What is the source for the four cups of wine [at the Passover Seder]?... Rabbi Yehoshua ben Levi said: They correspond to the four cups of Pharaoh [i.e. the four times Pharaoh's cup is mentioned in the cupbearer's dream].

The Brazen Bird

TEXT 7A

Ohel Yaakov, cited in Imrot Tehorot p. 425

הסבר יפה בדרך משל נותן המגיד מדובנא לשאלה, מניין ידע יוסף
לפתור את חלומו של שר המשקים לטוב ושל שר האופים לרע. הרי,
לכאורה, התוכן של שניהם אחד הוא. המשיל המגיד משל לתמונה
שהיה מצויר עליה אדם הנושא סל לחם על ראשו. עמדה ציפור חיה על
התמונה והתחילה לנקר במקורה על "הלחם" שבסל. עברו שני אנשים

והסתכלו בדבר. אמר אחד לחברו: הצייר של התמונה אמן גדול הוא; הציור טבעי כל-כך שאין הצפור מבחינה, וחושבת את "הלחם" שבסל ללחם ממש. אמר לו חברו: לא כי, אין הוא אמן גדול, כי רק את הלחם הצליח לצייר כטבעי ו"חי", אבל לא את האדם, והראיה—שאין הציפור מפחדת מפניו. אף כאן כך: כששמע יוסף את שר האופים מספר "והעוף אוכל אותם מן הסל מעל מעל ראשי" הבין יוסף שאין לפניו אדם חי אלא צל של אדם. על כן אמר לו "ובעוד שלשת ימים ישא פרעה את ראשך מעליך."

The Dubno Magid gives a nice parable to explain how Joseph knew to interpret the cupbearer's dream for the good and the baker's dream for bad, even though the two dreams seem to contain a similar message.

There was once a painting of a man with a basket of bread on his head. A live bird swooped down to the picture and began to peck at the "bread" in the basket. Two men passing by stopped to marvel at the sight. The first man said, "This painter is so talented—his painting looks so real that the bird thinks the bread is real!"

His friend replied, "He is not so talented, for he only managed to make the bread look real, but not the person. If the person would look real, the bird would be afraid to approach him."

So, too, here: When Joseph heard the baker say, "The birds were eating them from the basket atop my head," he realized that standing before him is essentially a *dead person, a shadow. Therefore, he said to him, "In three days, Pharaoh will remove your head from you."*

The Baker's Undoing

TEXT 7B

Me'asher Shmeina Lachmo, cited in Imrot Tehorot ibid.

שר המשקים ראה בחלומו, שהוא פעיל, עושה בידיו מתנוֹעע ופועל כאיש חי. כנאמר "וכוס פרעה בידי ואקח את הענבים ואשחט אותם ואתן את הכוס". כל הפעולות הללו מוכיחות על אדם חי ובעל מעשים, מכאן ראה יוסף שהוא איש חי, ולכן פתר לו לטוב.

אבל שר האופים לא ראה בחלומו שהוא עושה איזו פעולה, אלא שהכל נעשה בו, והוא כמת אשר איננו פועל ואינו עושה מאומה "והעוף אוכל אותם מן הסל מעל ראשי", מכאן הבין יוסף שהוא כאדם מת, שגזר דינו למות.

In the butler's dream, he was active, doing something with his own hands and moving like a live person. As the verse states, "Pharaoh's cup was in my hand, and I took the grapes and squeezed them into Pharaoh's cup." These actions reflect a live person capable of action. Therefore, Joseph knew this man was destined to live, and interpreted his dream accordingly.

But the baker did nothing in his dream. Instead, everything happened to him, like a dead person who cannot do a thing—"The birds were eating them from *the basket atop my head." Thus Joseph knew that this man was destined to die.*

CHART 1

The Baker's Dream	The Butler's Dream
Me too! In my dream…	*In my dream*
Behold, there were three wicker baskets on my head	*Behold, a vine is before me*
The work of a baker	*The cup of Pharaoh is in my hand* *I took the grapes* *I squeezed them into Pharaoh's cup*
And the birds were eating them from the basket atop my head.	*And I placed the cup on Pharoah's palm*

A Call to Action

Act, Don't Sigh

TEXT 8

Hayom Yom
In 1942, Rabbi Yosef Y. Schneersohn, the sixth rebbe of Chabad, gave his son-in-law, the future Rebbe, the task of compiling an anthology of Chasidic aphorisms and customs arranged according to the days of the year. In describing the completed product, Rabbi Yosef Yitschak wrote that it is "a book that is small in format but bursting with pearls and diamonds of the choicest quality."

The Lubavitcher Rebbe, Hayom Yom 22 Tevet

בַּאֲנָחוֹת לְבָד לֹא נִוָּשֵׁעַ. הָאֲנָחָה הִיא רַק כַּפַּת הַמַּנְעוּל לִפְתּוֹחַ אֶת הַלֵּב וְלִפְקוֹחַ אֶת הָעֵינַיִם שֶׁלֹּא לָשֶׁבֶת בְּחִבּוּק יָדַיִם, רַק לְסַדֵּר עֲבוֹדָה וּפוֹעַל, אִישׁ אִישׁ בַּאֲשֶׁר יוּכַל לִפְעוֹל וְלַעֲשׂוֹת בְּתַעֲמוּלָה לְחִזּוּק הַתּוֹרָה הַרְבָּצַת הַתּוֹרָה וּשְׁמִירַת הַמִּצְוֹת, זֶה בְּכִתְבוֹ וְזֶה בִּנְאוּמוֹ וְזֶה בְּכַסְפּוֹ.

Sighing alone will not bring us salvation. Sighing is only a doorknob that unlocks the heart and opens the eyes so that one will not sit idly with folded arms.

Instead, one should plan one's efforts and take action, every individual according to his abilities, toward the goal of buttressing and disseminating the study of Torah and the observance of its mitzvos: one person through writing, another one through public speaking, and another with his financial resources.

Tackling Life's Challenges

TEXT 9

The Lubavitcher Rebbe, Hayom Yom 8 Adar II

אַאמו״ר כּוֹתֵב בְּאֶחָד מִמִּכְתָּבָיו: טוֹבָה פְּעוּלָה אַחַת מֵאֶלֶף אֲנָחוֹת. אֱלֹקֵינוּ חַי וְתוֹרָה וּמִצְוֹת נִצְחִיִּים הֵמָּה, עֲזֹב אֶת הָאֲנָחָה וּשְׁקֹד בַּעֲבוֹדָה בְּפוֹעַל וִיחָנְךָ הָאֱלֹקִים.

My revered father, the Rebbe [Rashab], writes in one of his letters: "One action is better than a thousand sighs. Our G-d is alive and the Torah and its mitzvot are eternal. Abandon sighing, apply yourself diligently to actual avodah, and G-d will be gracious to you."

STORY

Once, Rabbi Yechezkel Feigin, affectionately known among his fellow *chasidim* as "Chatshe," was holding a *farbrengen* with *yeshivah* students in a cellar in Communist Russia. Needless to say, such a gathering was illegal, and two of the students were charged with the task of waiting upstairs to be on the lookout for anything suspicious.

Without any thought of the danger involved, Reb Chatshe *farbrenged* from the heart. He made demands of himself, and of the young men with whom he was speaking. He demanded more sincerity, more commitment. The *bachurim* understood and took his words to heart. Some were moved to tears.

Suddenly, one of the young watchmen upstairs rushed into

---

the cellar. A suspicious-looking group of men had entered the neighborhood. It was possible that they were KGB agents.

Immediately the atmosphere changed. The *bachurim* quickly suggested various plans. Some thought that they should all flee. Others argued that this would arouse suspicion and it was likely that several would be caught. It would be better, they continued, to take out magazines and political science books and pretend they were discussing current events. A third group maintained that the ruse would not help. Instead, they suggested hiding within the building. There was a sub-basement and several closets where they might not be found. The discussion soon became heated, each one defending his suggestions.

Then the other young watchman came down to tell them that the suspicious-looking group had left—the *farbrengen* could continue.

Reb Chatshe told his students, "Your conduct raises a question." They listened as he continued. "Which is more important to you—material things or spiritual things?" They were honest, and answered immediately, "Material things."

"Why, then," Reb Chatshe asked, "when I spoke to you about spiritual things, you begin to cry, but when a problem arose about our safety, no one cried?"

"What would crying have helped?" one of them asked. "Something had to be done."

"Oh, I see," Reb Chatshe responded, "crying is for when you know that you're not going to do anything about a problem..."

Producing Results

TEXT 10

The Lubavitcher Rebbe, Torat Menachem 5716 vol. 1 p. 152

כבוד קדושת מורי וחמי אדמו"ר... לא היה גורס "אנחות", ומה גם שזהו היפך דרך החסידות.

וטעם הדבר:

כל זמן שהנשמה בקרבי, ישנה השליחות שהטיל הקדוש ברוך הוא על כל אחד ואחת מישראל, בנתנו לו מספר מוגבל של ימים–"ימים יוצרו ולו אחד בהם–בשביל למלא שליחות זו, ובמילא, כשם ש"כל מה שברא הקדוש ברוך הוא בעולמו לא ברא דבר אחד לבטלה"... כמו כן אין גם זמן מיותר (לבטלה), כך שצריך לנצל כל יום וכל רגע כדבעי – כדברי כבוד קדושת מורי וחמי אדמו"ר בשם הצמח צדק: "אנן פועלי דיממי אנן" כלומר, התפקיד שלנו הוא להאיר.

ולכן אומר כבוד קדושת מורי וחמי אדמו"ר, "טובה פעולה אחת יותר מאלף אנחות":

אפילו אם יתאנח אלף אנחות, ויתאנח באמת–מוטב שיעשה פעולה אחת בעניני תורה ומצוות, וישכח מאלף האנחות, כי, אין הכוונה בשברון הגוף על ידי "אנחה (ש)שוברת חצי גופו (או "כל גופו") של אדם", שצריך לעבוד את ה' ביחד עם הגוף... וכאמור, שהתפקיד הוא להאיר ("פועלי דיממי")–תחילה בעצמו, בגופו ונפשו הבהמית, וגם בביתו, אצל אשתו וילדיו... שעל ידי זה מאיר בד' אמותיו, ולאחר זה– או בבת אחת–יוצאים גם להאיר בחלקו בעולם, ובמילא... "לאנחות" – בודאי לא.

My father-in-law the Rebbe… did not reckon with sighs, for sighing is contrary to the path of Chasidus.

The reason for this is that as long as the soul is in the body, one has a mission from G-d, who allotted him a certain amount of days to fulfill that mission. Consequently, just as "G-d did not create a thing in this world for naught"... there is no such thing as extra time to waste. Every day and every second must be used properly, as my father-in-law the Rebbe said in the name of the Tzemach Tzedek, "We are day workers," i.e., our job is to brighten the world.

Therefore, my father-in-law the Rebbe said, "One action is better than a thousand sighs." Even if you sigh a thousand sighs—heartfelt sighs—it would still be better to do one act of Torah and mitzvot, and forget the thousand sighs. For the purpose is not to break the body through sighs. Rather, one must serve G-d with the body... As we said, a Jew's job is to brighten—first to brighten his own body and animal soul, his homes, and the lives of his wife and children... Doing so will brighten his own life, and at that point, automatically, there is certainly no reason to sigh.

TEXT 11

The Lubavitcher Rebbe, Hayom Yom 26 Cheshvan

הַדֶּרֶךְ הָאֲמִתִּי הוּא שֶׁצְּרִיכִים לָדַעַת מַהוּת עַצְמוֹ, בְּהַכָּרָה אֲמִתִּית בְּחֶסְרוֹנוֹת עַצְמוֹ וּבְמַעֲלוֹת עַצְמוֹ. וְכַאֲשֶׁר יוֹדְעִים אֶת הַחֶסְרוֹנוֹת — לְתַקְנָם בַּעֲבוֹדָה בְּפוֹעַל, וְלֹא לָצֵאת יְדֵי חוֹבָתוֹ בַּאֲנָחוֹת בִּלְבַד.

The true path demands that one recognize his true self, with a genuine acknowledgment of his shortcomings and virtues. And when he is aware of his shortcomings, he should correct them with actual work, and not discharge his obligation by merely sighing.

9

CHANUKAH

The Psychology of the Chanukah Candles

Behaviorism vs. Cognitivism

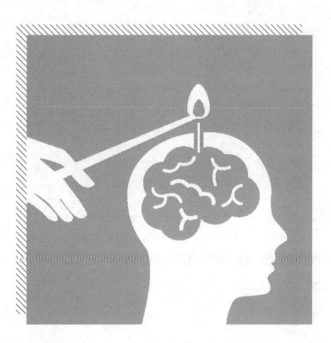

Dedicated in honor of the birthday of Reb Yaakov Cohen, 23 Kislev
May he and his family merit fulfillment of continuous blessings for health, happiness, nachas and success in all endeavors.

PARASHA OVERVIEW
Chanukah

Chanukah—the eight-day festival of light that begins on the eve of the 25th of the Jewish month of Kislev—celebrates the triumph of light over darkness, of purity over adulteration, of spirituality over materiality.

More than twenty-one centuries ago, the Holy Land was ruled by the Seleucids (Syrian-Greeks), who sought to forcefully Hellenize the people of Israel. Against all odds, a small band of faithful Jews defeated one of the mightiest armies on earth, drove the Greeks from the land, reclaimed the Holy Temple in Jerusalem and rededicated it to the service of G-d.

When they sought to light the Temple's menorah (the seven branched candelabrum), they found only a single cruse of olive oil that had escaped contamination by the Greeks; miraculously, the one-day supply burned for eight days, until new oil could be prepared under conditions of ritual purity.

To commemorate and publicize these miracles, the sages instituted the festival of Chanukah. At the heart of the festival is the nightly menorah (candelabrum) lighting: a single flame on the first night, two on the second evening, and so on till the eighth night of Chanukah, when all eight lights are kindled.

On Chanukah we also add the Hallel and Al HaNissim in our daily prayers to offer praise and thanksgiving to G-d for "delivering the strong into the hands of the weak, the many into the hands of the few... the wicked into the hands of the righteous."

Chanukah customs include eating foods fried in oil -- latkes (potato pancakes) and sufganiot (doughnuts); playing with the dreidel (a spinning top on which are inscribed the Hebrew letters nun, gimmel, hei and shin, an acronym for Nes Gadol Hayah Sham, "a great miracle happened there"); and the giving of Chanukah gelt, gifts of money, to children.

The Debate

How to Light

TEXT 1A

Talmud Tractate Shabbat 21b

תנו רבנן, מצות חנוכה נר איש וביתו. והמהדרין נר לכל אחד ואחד. והמהדרין מן המהדרין, בית שמאי אומרים, יום ראשון מדליק שמנה, מכאן ואילך פוחת והולך. ובית הלל אומרים, יום ראשון מדליק אחת, מכאן ואילך מוסיף והולך.

Babylonian Talmud

A literary work of monumental proportions that draws upon the legal, spiritual, intellectual, ethical, and historical traditions of Judaism. The 37 tractates of the Babylonian Talmud contain the teachings of the Jewish sages from the period after the destruction of the 2nd Temple through the 5th century CE. It has served as the primary vehicle for the transmission of the Oral Law and the education of Jews over the centuries; it is the entry point for all subsequent legal, ethical, and theological Jewish scholarship.

Our Rabbis taught: The mitzvah of Chanukah demands one light for a man and his household. Those who beautify the mitzvah kindle a light for each member of the household.

And concerning those who beautify it more than that, Beit Shammai says: On the first day light eight and after that gradually reduce; but Beit Hillel says: On the first day, one is lit, and thereafter they are progressively increased.

TEXT 1B

Ibid.

אמר עולא: פליגי בה תרי אמוראי במערבא, רבי יוסי בר אבין ורבי יוסי
בר זבידא. חד אמר, טעמא דבית שמאי כנגד ימים הנכנסין, וטעמא
דבית הלל כנגד ימים היוצאין.

וחד אמר, טעמא דבית שמאי כנגד פרי החג, וטעמא דבית הלל דמעלין
בקדש ואין מורידין.

*U*lla said: In Israel, two scholars—Rabbi Yosi the son of Avin and Rabbi Yosi the son of Zevida—argue. One maintains: The reason of Beit Shammai is that it should correspond to the days still to come, and the reason of Beit Hillel is that it should correspond to the days that have already passed.

But the other scholar maintains: Beit Shammai's reason is that it should correspond to the bulls offering of Sukkot, while Beit Hillel's reason is that we increase in matters of sanctity, but never decrease.

Divergent Paths

Stern vs. Compassionate

TEXT 2

Talmud Tractate Shabbat 31a

שוב מעשה בנכרי אחד שבא לפני שמאי, אמר לו: גיירני על מנת
שתלמדני כל התורה כולה כשאני עומד על רגל אחת. דחפו באמת
הבנין שבידו.

בא לפני הלל, גייריה. אמר לו: דעלך סני לחברך לא תעביד, זו היא כל
התורה כולה; ואידך, פירושה הוא, זיל גמור.

It happened that a certain non-Jew came before
Shammai and said to him, "Convert me on the
condition that you teach me the whole Torah while
I stand on one foot." Thereupon, he chased him away
with the builders' measuring tool that was in his hand.

The same fellow came before Hillel, and Hillel con-
verted him, saying, "That which is despicable to you,
do not do to your fellow; this is the whole Torah, and
the rest is commentary; go and learn it."

TEXT 3

Mishnah Tractate Ediyot 4:1

אלו דברים מקולי בית שמאי ומחומרי בית הלל ביצה שנולדה ביום
טוב בית שמאי אומרים תאכל ובית הלל אומרים לא תאכל בית שמאי
אומרים שאור בכזית וחמץ בככותבת ובית הלל אומרים זה וזה בכזית.

*T*he following are instances where Beit Shammai is more lenient and Beit Hillel is more
strict: An egg that was laid on a festival, Beit
Shammai says: It may be eaten. And Beit Hillel says:
It may not be eaten. Beit Shammai says: [A person is
liable for a violation of Passover-eating prohibitions]
with an olive-sized [portion] of yeast and a date-sized
[portion] of leavened product. Beit Hillel says: With
an olive-sized portion [each] of [yeast] and [leav-
ened product].

Mishnah
The first authoritative work of
Jewish law that was codified in
writing. The Mishnah contains
the oral traditions that were
passed down from teacher
to student; it supplements,
clarifies, and systematizes
the commandments of the
Torah. Due to the continual
persecution of the Jewish
people, it became increasingly
difficult to guarantee that
these traditions would not
be forgotten. Rabbi Yehudah
Hanasi therefore redacted
the Mishnah at the end of the
2nd century. It serves as the
foundation for the Talmud.

Champions of Halachah

TEXT 4

Talmud Tractate Eruvin 13b

אמר רבי אבא אמר שמואל: שלש שנים נחלקו בית שמאי ובית הלל,
הללו אומרים הלכה כמותנו והללו אומרים הלכה כמותנו.
יצאה בת קול ואמרה: אלו ואלו דברי אלהים חיים הן, והלכה כבית הלל.
וכי מאחר שאלו ואלו דברי אלהים חיים מפני מה זכו בית הלל לקבוע
הלכה כמותן? מפני שנוחין ועלובין היו, ושונין דבריהן ודברי בית שמאי.
ולא עוד אלא שמקדימין דברי בית שמאי לדבריהן.

For three years, the House of Hillel and the House of Shammai argued. One said, "The Halachah is like us," and the other said, "The Halachah is like us."

A Heavenly voice spoke, "These and these are the words of the living G-d, and the Halachah follows the House of Hillel."

A question was raised: Since the Heavenly voice declared, "Both these and those are the words of the Living G-d," why was the Halachah established to follow the opinion of Hillel?

It is because the students of Hillel were kind and gracious. They taught their own ideas as well as the ideas from the students of Shammai. Not only that, they went so far as to teach Shammai's opinions first.

Potential vs. Reality

TEXT 5

The Lubavitcher Rebbe, Likutei Sichot, vol. 6 p. 70

מען געפינט כמה וכמה פלוגתות צווישן בית שמאי און בית הלל, וואו
דער יסוד פון זייער מחלוקת באשטייט אין דעם, אז בית שמאי האלטן
"אזלינן בתר בכח" און בית הלל האלטן "אזלינן בתר בפועל".

We find many arguments between Beit Shammai and Beit Hillel where the fundamental dispute is this: Beit Shammai maintains that "we focus on the potential," whereas Beit Hillel counters that "we focus on the practical."

Rabbi Menachem Mendel Schneerson
1902–1994

The towering Jewish leader of the 20th century, known as "the Lubavitcher Rebbe," or simply as "the Rebbe." Born in southern Ukraine, the Rebbe escaped Nazi-occupied Europe, arriving in the U.S. in June 1941. The Rebbe inspired and guided the revival of traditional Judaism after the European devastation, impacting virtually every Jewish community the world over. The Rebbe often emphasized that the performance of just one additional good deed could usher in the era of Moshiach. The Rebbe's scholarly talks and writings have been printed in more than 200 volumes.

Example—Creation

TEXT 6

Talmud Tractate Eruvin 13b

תנו רבנן: שתי שנים ומחצה נחלקו בית שמאי ובית הלל. הללו אומרים:
נוח לו לאדם שלא נברא יותר משנברא, והללו אומרים: נוח לו לאדם
שנברא יותר משלא נברא.

Our Rabbis taught: For two and a half years, the school of Shammai and the school of Hillel were in dispute, the former asserting that it were better for man not to have been created than to have been created, and the latter maintaining that it is better for man to have been created than not to have been created.

TEXT 7

The Lubavitcher Rebbe, Sefer Hasichot 5748, vol. 2, p. 661-662

והנה פלוגתת בית שמאי ובית הלל—אי אזלינן בתר בכח או בתר
בפועל—מצינו גם בנוגע בריאת האדם: הללו (בית שמאי) אומרים נוח
לו לאדם שלא נברא יותר משנברא, והללו (בית הלל) אומרים נוח לו
לאדם שנברא יותר משלא נברא:

בריאת האדם פירושו כאן—ירידת נשמתו למטה.

ופלוגתת בית שמאי ובית הלל—אם בריאת האדם ירידת נשמתו למטה
היא נוח לו לאדם או לאו—היא דאזלי לשיטתייהו אי אזלינן בתר בכח
או בתר בפועל:

לשיטת בית שמאי שהעיקר הוא הבכח—בכדי שהאדם יגיע לשלימותו
אין הכרח שנשמתו תרד למטה ותעסוק בתורה ומצות בפועל מכיון
שגם בהיותה למעלה יש לה הכח על זה. וזה מה שירדה הנשמה למטה
שתעסוק בתורה ומצות בפועל הוא רק מפני שכן הוא רצון הקדוש
ברוך הוא.

ולכן סבירא ליה לבית שמאי נוח לו לאדם שלא נברא כו'—שהכוונה
בבריאת האדם (ירידת נשמתו למטה) היא בכדי להשלים רצון הקדוש
ברוך הוא, אבל בנוגע להאדם בתורה—נוח לו לאדם שלא נברא כו'.

מה שאין כן לשיטת בית הלל שהעיקר הוא הבפועל—בכדי שהאדם
יגיע לשלימותו הוא דוקא על ידי שנשמתו יורדת למטה ועוסקת
בתורה ומצות בפועל. ולכן סבירא ליה לבית הלל נוח לו לאדם שנברא
כו' דבריאת האדם היא (לא רק להשלים רצון הקדוש ברוך הוא, אלא
גם) טובת ושלימות האדם, נוח לו לאדם שנברא כו'.

> "**C**reation of man" in this context refers to the descent of the soul into the physical world.

The dispute of Beit Shammai and Beit Hillel is in accordance with their respective views about whether we measure by potential or by the actual.

According to Beit Shammai, for whom the potential is sufficient, in order for the soul to attain perfection there is no need for the soul to actually descend to this world and physically engage in Torah and mitzvot, *for even when it is on High, it has this potential [and merely having the requisite potential renders the soul complete]. The only reason why the soul actually descended to the physical world was because G-d so desired [but not for its own benefit].*

Thus, Beit Shammai maintains that it would be better for man not to be created, for the purpose of this creation (namely, the descent of the soul) is strictly to fulfill the will of G-d; but for the person, he or she would be better off without it.

Contrarily, according to Beit Hillel, who focuses on the actual—in order for man to attain perfection, his soul must actually descend into the material world, perform the physical mitzvot, *and study the Torah in its earthly form. Thus, Beit Hillel maintains that the soul is pleased with Creation, for the creation of man not only fulfills G-d's will, but it also benefits the soul itself.*

Example—Impurity of Honeycomb

TEXT 8

Mishnah Tractate Uktzin 3:11

חלות דבש מאימתי מיטמאות משום משקה בית שמאי אומרים משיחרחר, בית הלל אומרים משירסק.

eginning when do honeycombs become susceptible to being rendered impure as liquids?

Beit Shammai says: once one stirs it up [by smoking the bees out, or heating it]. And Beit Hillel says: once one breaks it apart [to remove the honey].

Soul Differences

TEXT 9

Rabbi Shneur Zalman of Liadi, Tanya, Iggeret Hakodesh, ch. 13

הנה בכלל עובדי השם יש ב' בחינות ומדרגות חלוקות מצד שורש נשמתם למעלה מבחינת ימין ושמאל, דהיינו שבחינת שמאל היא מדת הצמצום וההסתר בעבודת השם... והנה ממדה זו נמשכה גם כן בחינת הצמצום והגבול בעבודת ה' כמו בצדקה להיות נידון בהשג יד, והמבזבז אל יבזבז יותר מחומש, וכהאי גוונא בתלמוד תורה ושארי מצות—די לו שיוצא ידי חובתו מחיוב מפורש שחייבתו התורה בפירוש לקבוע עתים כו'.

אך בחינת ימין היא מדת החסד וההתפשטות בעבודת ה' בהתרחבות בלי צמצום והסתר כלל... ואין מעצור לרוח נדבתו בין בצדקה ובין בתלמוד תורה ושארי מצות ולא די לו לצאת ידי חובתו בלבד אלא עד בלי די כו'...

בית שמאי ששרש נשמתם מבחינת שמאל העליון, ולכן היו דנין
להחמיר תמיד בכל איסורי התורה. ובית הלל שהיו מבחינת ימין העליון
היו מלמדין זכות להקל ולהתיר איסורי בית שמאי.

**Rabbi Shneur
Zalman of Liadi**
(Alter Rebbe)
1745–1812
Chasidic rebbe, halachic
authority, and founder of
the Chabad movement. The
Alter Rebbe was born in
Liozna, Belarus, and was
among the principal students
of the Magid of Mezeritch.
His numerous works include
the *Tanya*, an early classic
containing the fundamentals
of Chabad Chasidism, and
Shulchan Aruch HaRav,
an expanded and reworked
code of Jewish law.

Among Divine servants, there are two degrees and levels which, depending on the root of their souls above, are distinct in relation to the categories of the right and the left.

That is, the characteristic of the left is the trait of contraction (tzimtzum) and concealment in Divine service... From this attribute derives also the aspect of contraction (tzimtzum) and limitation in Divine service; for example, with charity—to judge according to the means, "And he who expends should not expend more than one fifth"; and, likewise, as regards the study of Torah and the other commandments—he makes do with discharging his duty, the definite duty to which the Torah obliges him, "to appoint times ..."

By contrast, the characteristic of the right is the attribute of grace (chesed) and extension in Divine service by way of expansion, without any contraction and concealment whatsoever... There is no restraint to the spirit of his generosity—whether it be with respect to charity, the study of Torah, or other commandments. He does not suffice in discharging his obligation only, but to the extent of "never sufficient..."

The root of Beit Shammai's soul is of the category of the supernal left—that is why they always decided stringently as regards all the prohibitions of the Torah. But Beit Hillel, who were of the supernal right, would find favorable arguments to be lenient and to permit the injunctions of Beit Shammai.

TEXT 10

The Lubavitcher Rebbe, Likutei Sichot vol. 6 p. 78

בית שמאי איז שרשם פון גבורות, און בית הלל איז שרשם פון חסדים (וואס דערפאר זיינען בית שמאי מחמיר און בית הלל מקילי). און היות אז גבורה איז בחינת "העלם" און חסד איז "גילוי", דעריבער האלטן בית שמאי אז דער עיקר איז דער "בכח" און בית הלל האלטן אז דער עיקר איז דער "בפועל"—ווייל כח איז ענינו העלם און פועל—גילוי.

The root of Beit Shammai's soul is in the Supernal attribute of gevurah, and Beit Hillel is rooted in chesed (thus, Beit Shammai is stricter and Beit Hillel is more lenient). Gevurah is generally associated with "concealment" while chesed is generally associated with "revelation." Accordingly, Beit Shammai focuses on the potential and Beit Hillel focuses on the practical—for potential is the concealed state, while practical is the revealed state.

Dealing with Darkness

How Do We Deal with Darkness?

TEXT 11A

The Lubavitcher Rebbe, Igrot Kodesh, vol. 1, p. 80

ולכן מי שיצר הרע טימא את מקדשו ובא ליטהר ולהכנס תחת כנפות
השכינה, הנה לבית שמאי חילת ועיקר העבודה הוא בסור מרע, ובערת
הרע מקרבך. וכשמתחיל בעבודה הרע בתוקפו, ונזקק ליגיעה גדולה
ואור רב ודורשין ממנו יגיעה כזו, אבל מיום ליום הרע פוחת והולך
ובמילא אין צריך לאור גדול כביום א׳.

For some, the Yetzer Hara *may have contaminated his inner Sanctuary, and he now wishes to purify himself and enter under the canopy of Divine grace. According to Beit Shammai, the first thing he must do is to move away from negativity, to "remove the evil from your midst."*

When starting out, the evil is in its full strength and therefore warrants supreme effort and abundant light. As the days progress, the evil decreases and thus less light is needed.

The Bulls

TEXT 11B

Ibid.

ודוגמא לזה: פרי החג שמקריבים אותם כנגד אומות העולם שלא יצדה
(לשון צדיא ורקניא) העולם מהם, אלא יהפכו לטוב ומיום ליום פוחת
והולך הרע שבהם ולכן אין צריך כבר למספר קרבנות גדול כל כך...

An example of this are the sacrifices offered on the days of Sukkot. These sacrifices correspond to the nations of the world, namely that the world should not be "trapped" by their negativity, rather they should be transformed to the good. Each day, their negativity is diminished [through this process of transformation], and thus, we no longer need such a large number of sacrifices.

Hillel's Approach

TEXT 11C

Ibid.

אבל בית הלל אומרים שתחילת הכל צריך להכנס תחת כנפי השכינה
אף שעדיין הרע בתוקפו אצלו, ויתחיל בעבודתו בעניינים שלו עשה
טוב, עבודה בקדש ממש ומצוה ומצוה גוררת מצוה, ומעלין בקדש, שמעט
מעט יוסיף אומץ להיות מוסיף והולך.

Beit Hillel, however, holds that first one must en-
ter the canopy of holiness, despite the fact that
the evil is prevalent inside him. He should begin
Divine service by doing good things. And "one mitzvah
leads to another," ascending in holiness, little by little
gaining strength, until the evil is completely eradicated.

STORY

The Alter Rebbe, Rabbi Shneur Zalman of Liadi, once took leave from his master, the Maggid of Mezritch. The Maggid's son, Rabbi Avraham—"The Angel" as he was called—came out to bid farewell to his friend and student. Sitting on the wagon, the Alter Rebbe was examining the horses that were to take him on the journey home. Rabbi Avraham, who barely had a foot in this physical world, hence his title "angel," called out to the Alter Rebbe:

"G o , "פָאר פָאה, קוק נישט אויף די פֶערד" go! Stop looking at the horses!"

Chasidim interpreted this as a directive in life: In life you don't always have the luxury to dissect your inner horse, the beast that lurks inside your psyche. You must continue the journey!

The Verdict

TEXT 12

Rabbi Yosef Caro
(Maran, *Beit Yosef*)
1488–1575

Halachic authority and author.
Rabbi Caro was born in Spain,
but was forced to flee during
the expulsion in 1492 and
eventually settled in Safed,
Israel. He authored many
works including the *Beit Yosef*,
Kesef Mishneh, and a mystical
work, *Magid Meisharim*.
Rabbi Caro's magnum opus,
the Shulchan Aruch (Code
of Jewish Law), has been
universally accepted as the
basis for modern Jewish law.

Rabbi Yosef Caro, Shulchan Aruch, Orach Chayim 671:2

כמה נרות מדליק? בלילה הראשון מדליק אחד, מכאן ואילך מוסיף
והולך אחד בכל לילה, עד שבליל אחרון יהיו שמונה. ואפילו אם רבים
בני הבית לא ידליקו יותר.

How many candles should one light? On the first night, one, from then on add one each night, finishing with eight on the final night. Even if there are many members in the house, one should not light more.

STORY: YOU'RE SELFISH?

Rabbi Manis Freidman, dean of Beit Chana Women's Seminary in Minneapolis, tells the story of a young Jewish woman in Minnesota who wanted to marry but was unsuccessful because she was self-centered. Whenever she met a man, she only spoke about herself.

She was seeing one psychologist after another, who all analyzed her past and diagnosed her as a classic narcissist, who saw the entire world around her as a mirror. They explained to her all of the psychological reasons governing her behavior. They explained to her how this flaw stemmed from the primal formations of her psyche (they probably explained that her mother got this from her mother, and so on, all the way back to Chavah, who ate from the tree ...), and this is why she was afraid to open up to people.

But after all the therapy, she was not helped. She still could not manage to change her behavior. Rabbi Manis Friedman suggested that she consult with the Rebbe.

She presented a sheaf of papers to the Rebbe with the analyses of her doctors, and said, "These are my problems."

The Rebbe, who was a speed reader, leafed through the stack of papers within moments. Then he put them down. She figured that he had politely glanced through the papers but hadn't read them. The Rebbe said, "Okay, so what's the problem?"

Stunned by this, she said, "What?!"

The Rebbe said, "I don't understand the problem."

"Did you read it?" she asked.

"Yes, I read it," said the Rebbe.

"What do you mean—there's no problem? I've been in therapy for years and psychologists have made hundreds of dollars off me every week. How can you say there's no problem? I'm self-centered!"

The Rebbe said, "I hear, but I don't understand the problem!"

She began telling the Rebbe about her mother and grandmother and the Rebbe said, "I'm not asking for your history now. That's written here. I'm asking you what your problem is NOW."

She said, "The problem is that I'm self-centered. I'm completely egotistic. I have no space for others. I can't let anyone in my life. It's ruining my life! I'm just simply selfish."

"So, stop being selfish!" said the Rebbe.

She looked at the Rebbe as though to say, "Is this what I came to hear?"

The Rebbe went on. "If you'll listen to me, when you go back to your school and you're in the dining room, you'll offer to bring to the girls sitting and eating whatever they need for their meal. Do this at every meal." She told the Rebbe that this behavior was impossible for her. The Rebbe said, "This is what it means to think about someone else."

She went back to Minnesota and listened to the Rebbe's advice. The other girls responded positively to her overtures and within weeks her relationships were transformed. Today she is married and has a beautiful family.

You want to stop being selfish? You don't always have to analyze it for years. Just do favors for people! Do one favor a day for a person and you will stop being selfish.

10

VAYIGASH

My Brother's Keeper

Mutual Responsibility in Judaism

Dedicated by the JLI team in honor of the Bar Mitzvah of Hatamim Avraham Ze'ev Mintz, 22 Elul 5776
May he continue to bring much nachas to his parents, family, and Klal Yisroel.

PARASHA OVERVIEW
Vayigash

Judah approaches Joseph to plead for the release of Benjamin, offering himself as a slave to the Egyptian ruler in Benjamin's stead. Upon witnessing his brothers' loyalty to one another, Joseph reveals his identity to them. "I am Joseph," he declares. "Is my father still alive?"

The brothers are overcome by shame and remorse, but Joseph comforts them. "It was not you who sent me here," he says to them, "but G-d. It has all been ordained from Above to save us, and the entire region, from famine."

The brothers rush back to Canaan with the news. Jacob comes to Egypt with his sons and their families—seventy souls in all—and is reunited with his beloved son after 22 years. On his way to Egypt he receives the divine promise: "Fear not to go down to Egypt; for I will there make of you a great nation. I will go down with you into Egypt, and I will also surely bring you up again."

Joseph gathers the wealth of Egypt by selling food and seed during the famine. Pharaoh gives Jacob's family the fertile county of Goshen to settle, and the children of Israel prosper in their Egyptian exile.

Judah and Yosef

The Big Reveal

TEXT 1A

Bereishit (Genesis) 44:4-13

הֵם יָצְאוּ אֶת הָעִיר לֹא הִרְחִיקוּ וְיוֹסֵף אָמַר לַאֲשֶׁר עַל בֵּיתוֹ קוּם רְדֹף אַחֲרֵי הָאֲנָשִׁים וְהִשַּׂגְתָּם וְאָמַרְתָּ אֲלֵהֶם לָמָּה שִׁלַּמְתֶּם רָעָה תַּחַת טוֹבָה:

הֲלוֹא זֶה אֲשֶׁר יִשְׁתֶּה אֲדֹנִי בּוֹ וְהוּא נַחֵשׁ יְנַחֵשׁ בּוֹ הֲרֵעֹתֶם אֲשֶׁר עֲשִׂיתֶם:

וַיַּשִּׂגֵם וַיְדַבֵּר אֲלֵהֶם אֶת הַדְּבָרִים הָאֵלֶּה:

וַיֹּאמְרוּ אֵלָיו לָמָּה יְדַבֵּר אֲדֹנִי כַּדְּבָרִים הָאֵלֶּה חָלִילָה לַעֲבָדֶיךָ מֵעֲשׂוֹת כַּדָּבָר הַזֶּה:

הֵן כֶּסֶף אֲשֶׁר מָצָאנוּ בְּפִי אַמְתְּחֹתֵינוּ הֱשִׁיבֹנוּ אֵלֶיךָ מֵאֶרֶץ כְּנָעַן וְאֵיךְ נִגְנֹב מִבֵּית אֲדֹנֶיךָ כֶּסֶף אוֹ זָהָב:

אֲשֶׁר יִמָּצֵא אִתּוֹ מֵעֲבָדֶיךָ וָמֵת וְגַם אֲנַחְנוּ נִהְיֶה לַאדֹנִי לַעֲבָדִים:

וַיֹּאמֶר גַּם עַתָּה כְדִבְרֵיכֶם כֶּן הוּא אֲשֶׁר יִמָּצֵא אִתּוֹ יִהְיֶה לִּי עָבֶד וְאַתֶּם תִּהְיוּ נְקִיִּם:

וַיְמַהֲרוּ וַיּוֹרִדוּ אִישׁ אֶת אַמְתַּחְתּוֹ אָרְצָה וַיִּפְתְּחוּ אִישׁ אַמְתַּחְתּוֹ:

וַיְחַפֵּשׂ בַּגָּדוֹל הֵחֵל וּבַקָּטֹן כִּלָּה וַיִּמָּצֵא הַגָּבִיעַ בְּאַמְתַּחַת בִּנְיָמִן:

וַיִּקְרְעוּ שִׂמְלֹתָם וַיַּעֲמֹס אִישׁ עַל חֲמֹרוֹ וַיָּשֻׁבוּ הָעִירָה:

They had just left the city and had not gone far, when Joseph said to his steward, "Up, go after the men! And when you overtake them, say to them, 'Why did you repay good with evil?

"It is the very one from which my master drinks and which he uses for divination. It was a wicked thing for you to do!'"

He overtook them and spoke those words to them.

And they said to him, "Why does my lord say such things? Far be it from your servants to do anything of the kind!

"Here we brought back to you from the land of Canaan the money that we found in the mouths of our bags. How, then, could we have stolen any silver or gold from your master's house?

"Whichever of your servants it is found with shall die; the rest of us, moreover, shall become slaves to my lord."

He replied, "Although what you are proposing is right, only the one with whom it is found shall be my slave; but the rest of you shall go free."

So each one hastened to lower his bag to the ground, and each one opened his bag.

He searched, beginning with the oldest and ending with the youngest; and the goblet turned up in Benjamin's bag.

At this, they rent their clothes. Each reloaded his pack animal, and they returned to the city.

TEXT 1B

Ibid., 44:17

וַיֹּאמֶר חָלִילָה לִּי מֵעֲשׂוֹת זֹאת הָאִישׁ אֲשֶׁר נִמְצָא הַגָּבִיעַ בְּיָדוֹ הוּא יִהְיֶה
לִּי עָבֶד וְאַתֶּם עֲלוּ לְשָׁלוֹם אֶל אֲבִיכֶם:

B ut he replied, "Far be it from me to act thus! Only he in whose possession the goblet was found shall be my slave; the rest of you go back in peace to your father."

TEXT 2A

Ibid., 44:18

וַיִּגַּשׁ אֵלָיו יְהוּדָה וַיֹּאמֶר בִּי אֲדֹנִי יְדַבֶּר נָא עַבְדְּךָ דָבָר בְּאָזְנֵי אֲדֹנִי וְאַל יִחַר
אַפְּךָ בְּעַבְדֶּךָ כִּי כָמוֹךָ כְּפַרְעֹה:

T hen Judah went up to him and said, "Please, my lord, let your servant appeal to my lord, and do not be impatient with your servant, you who are the equal of Pharaoh."

TEXT 2B

Ibid., 44:30-34

וְעַתָּה כְּבֹאִי אֶל עַבְדְּךָ אָבִי וְהַנַּעַר אֵינֶנּוּ אִתָּנוּ וְנַפְשׁוֹ קְשׁוּרָה בְנַפְשׁוֹ:

וְהָיָה כִּרְאוֹתוֹ כִּי אֵין הַנַּעַר וָמֵת וְהוֹרִידוּ עֲבָדֶיךָ אֶת שֵׂיבַת עַבְדְּךָ אָבִינוּ בְּיָגוֹן שְׁאֹלָה:

כִּי עַבְדְּךָ עָרַב אֶת הַנַּעַר מֵעִם אָבִי לֵאמֹר אִם לֹא אֲבִיאֶנּוּ אֵלֶיךָ וְחָטָאתִי לְאָבִי כָּל הַיָּמִים:

וְעַתָּה יֵשֶׁב נָא עַבְדְּךָ תַּחַת הַנַּעַר עֶבֶד לַאדֹנִי וְהַנַּעַר יַעַל עִם אֶחָיו:

כִּי אֵיךְ אֶעֱלֶה אֶל אָבִי וְהַנַּעַר אֵינֶנּוּ אִתִּי פֶּן אֶרְאֶה בָרָע אֲשֶׁר יִמְצָא אֶת אָבִי:

"**N**ow, if I come to your servant my father and the boy is not with us—since his own life is so bound up with his.

"*When he sees that the boy is not with us, he will die, and your servants will send the white head of your servant our father down to Sheol in grief.*

"*Now your servant has pledged himself for the boy to my father, saying, 'If I do not bring him back to you, I shall stand guilty before my father forever.'*

"*Therefore, please let your servant remain as a slave to my lord instead of the boy, and let the boy go back with his brothers.*

"*For how can I go back to my father unless the boy is with me? Let me not be witness to the woe that would overtake my father!*"

A Personal Guarantee

TEXT 2C

Ibid., 44:32

כִּי עַבְדְּךָ עָרַב אֶת הַנַּעַר מֵעִם אָבִי לֵאמֹר אִם לֹא אֲבִיאֶנּוּ אֵלֶיךָ וְחָטָאתִי
לְאָבִי כָּל הַיָּמִים:

For your servant assumed responsibility for the boy from my father, saying, "If I do not bring him to you, I will have sinned against my father forever."

TEXT 3

Ibid., 43:8-9

וַיֹּאמֶר יְהוּדָה אֶל יִשְׂרָאֵל אָבִיו שִׁלְחָה הַנַּעַר אִתִּי וְנָקוּמָה וְנֵלֵכָה וְנִחְיֶה
וְלֹא נָמוּת גַּם אֲנַחְנוּ גַם אַתָּה גַּם טַפֵּנוּ:
אָנֹכִי אֶעֶרְבֶנּוּ מִיָּדִי תְּבַקְשֶׁנּוּ אִם לֹא הֲבִיאֹתִיו אֵלֶיךָ וְהִצַּגְתִּיו לְפָנֶיךָ
וְחָטָאתִי לְךָ כָּל הַיָּמִים:

And Judah said to Israel, his father, "Send the lad with me, and we will get up and go, and we will live and not die, both we and you and also our young children.

"I will guarantee him; from my hand you can demand him. If I do not bring him to you and stand him up before you, I will have sinned against you forever."

TEXT 4

Midrash Tanchuma, Vayigash §5

אמר לו יוסף יהודה למה אתה דבן מכל אחיך ואני רואה בגביע שיש
באחיך גדולים ממך ואתה פטיט?

אמר לו כל זאת שאתה רואה בשביל הערבות שערבתי אותו.

Josef said to Judah, "And why, of all of your brothers, have you become the spokesman? I can divine with my goblet that there are amongst you brothers some who are older than you, and nevertheless you are speaking up."

He replied, "Everything that you see is on account of the responsibility I assumed for him."

Midrash Tanchuma

A midrashic work bearing the name of Rabbi Tanchuma, a 4th century Talmudic sage quoted often in this work. Midrash is the designation of a particular genre of rabbinic literature usually forming a running commentary on specific books of the Bible. *Midrash Tanchuma* provides textual exegeses, expounds upon the biblical narrative, and develops and illustrates moral principles. *Tanchuma* is unique in that many of its sections commence with a halachic discussion, which subsequently leads into non-halachic teachings.

Bondsmen, Guarantors, and Legal Responsibility

TEXT 5A

Mishnah, Tractate Baba Batra 10:7

המלוה את חבירו על ידי ערב. לא יפרע מן הערב. ואם אמר על מנת
שאפרע ממי שארצה. יפרע מן הערב. רבן שמעון בן גמליאל אומר אם
יש נכסים ללוה בין כך ובין כך לא יפרע מן הערב.

One who loaned money to his fellow on a guarantor's security may not exact payment from the guarantor. But if he had said, "On

Mishnah

The first authoritative work of Jewish law that was codified in writing. The Mishnah contains the oral traditions that were passed down from teacher to student; it supplements, clarifies, and systematizes the commandments of the Torah. Due to the continual persecution of the Jewish people, it became increasingly difficult to guarantee that these traditions would not be forgotten. Rabbi Judah Hanasi therefore redacted the Mishnah at the end of the 2nd century. It serves as the foundation for the Talmud.

the condition that I may exact payment from whom I wish," then he may exact payment from the guarantor.

Rabban Shimon ben Gamliel says: If the borrower had property, [whether he made the condition] or not, he may not exact payment from the guarantor.

TEXT 5B

Rabbi Shmuel ben Meir, Rashbam,
Talmud Tractate Baba Batra 173a

"לא יפרע מן הערב". תחלה עד שיתבע את הלוה לדין ויחייבוהו בית דין. ואם אין לו מה לשלם, אז יפרע מן הערב. הכי מפרשינן לה בגמרא במסקנא.

Rabbi Shmuel ben Meir (Rashbam)
1085–1158
Talmudist and biblical commentator. Rashbam was born in Troyes, France, to Yocheved, the daughter of Rashi. Rashbam, a prominent member of the Tosafists, authored commentaries on the Pentateuch and the Talmud. Like his grandfather's, Rashbam's commentaries focus on the plain meaning of the Talmudic and biblical texts.

"He may not exact payment from the guarantor." —At first. Only if he first demands payment from the borrower, who is then found to be a debtor in a court of law. If the borrower then cannot pay, the lender can exact payment from the guarantor, as the Talmud later explains [the teaching of the Mishnah] in its conclusion.

TEXT 5C

Talmud Tractate Bava Batra 173b

אמר רבי הונא מנין לערב דמשתעבד?

דכתיב "אנכי אערבנו מידי תבקשנו".

*R*abbi Huna said: From where [is the law derived] that a guarantor becomes financially obligated?

[The source] is as it is written, "I will guarantee him; from my hand you can demand him."

Babylonian Talmud
A literary work of monumental proportions that draws upon the legal, spiritual, intellectual, ethical, and historical traditions of Judaism. The 37 tractates of the Babylonian Talmud contain the teachings of the Jewish sages from the period after the destruction of the 2nd Temple through the 5th century CE. It has served as the primary vehicle for the transmission of the Oral Law and the education of Jews over the centuries; it is the entry point for all subsequent legal, ethical, and theological Jewish scholarship.

Exegetical Overreach?

TEXT 6

Rabbi Naftali Tzvi Yehuda Berlin,
Ha'amek She'elah on Sheiltot, She'ilta 31:2

ותו מאי ראיה מהשתעבדות לשמור ולהשיב דבר שהוא בעין
להשתעבדות על מלוה דבר שאינו בעין?

*A*nother question: What evidence can be brought from the assumed obligation to protect and return something currently in existence, to the assumed obligation for a loan that is no longer extant?

Anatomy of the *Arev*

Personal or Financial

TEXT 7

The Lubavitcher Rebbe, Likutei Sichot, vol. 30, p. 216

שעבודו של ערב יש לבארו בשני אופנים: א) השעבוד שייך רק להחוב,
דמשעבד נפשיה לשלם חובו של הלוה, ב) הערב עומד במקום הלוה,
ולכן שעבוד הגוף שעל הלוה לשלם חובו (ופריעת בעל חוב מצוה), חל
על הערב (העומד במקומו).

Rabbi Menachem Mendel Schneerson
1902–1994

The towering Jewish leader of the 20th century, known as "the Lubavitcher Rebbe," or simply as "the Rebbe." Born in southern Ukraine, the Rebbe escaped Nazi-occupied Europe, arriving in the U.S. in June 1941. The Rebbe inspired and guided the revival of traditional Judaism after the European devastation, impacting virtually every Jewish community the world over. The Rebbe often emphasized that the performance of just one additional good deed could usher in the era of Moshiach. The Rebbe's scholarly talks and writings have been printed in more than 200 volumes.

The guarantor's liability can be explained in two ways:

1. His liability applies only to the **debt**, [such that the guarantor] commits himself to pay the borrower's debt.

2. The arev assumes the place of the [**person**] of the borrower; therefore, the borrower's personal obligation to repay his debt, (and the mitzvah associated with doing so,) now falls on the guarantor (who is now standing in the place of the borrower).

Benediction Bondsman

TEXT 8

Talmud Tractate Shavuot 39a

כל ישראל ערבים זה בזה.

All of Israel are guarantors for one another.

TEXT 9

Rabbi Shneur Zalman of Liadi, Shulchan Aruch, Orach Chaim, 167:23

אַף מִי שֶׁאֵינוֹ מְחוּיָב בַּדָּבָר מִפְּנֵי שֶׁכְּבָר יָצָא יְדֵי חוֹבָתוֹ יָכוֹל לְבָרֵךְ לְמִי שֶׁעֲדַיִין לֹא יָצָא וְאֵינוֹ יוֹדֵעַ לְבָרֵךְ לְעַצְמוֹ כְּגוֹן לְקַדֵּשׁ קִידּוּשׁ הַיּוֹם לְנָשִׁים וְעַמֵּי הָאָרֶץ. לְפִי שֶׁבְּמִצְוֹת שֶׁהֵן חוֹבָה כָּל יִשְׂרָאֵל עֲרֵבִים זֶה בָּזֶה, וְגַם הוּא נִקְרָא מְחוּיָב בַּדָּבָר כְּשֶׁחֲבֵירוֹ לֹא יָצָא יְדֵי חוֹבָתוֹ עֲדַיִין.

One who has already discharged his mitzvah obligation is no longer obligated to fulfill that mitzvah. However, if another person is not familiar with the mitzvah, e.g., he cannot make Kiddush himself, the former person may recite the blessing on behalf of the latter. The reason for this is because all Jews are responsible for one another.

For example, [he can] sanctify [the Shabbat day] with Kiddush [for someone else] because for a mitzvah incumbent upon all Israel, each person is the other's

Rabbi Shneur Zalman of Liadi
(Alter Rebbe)
1745–1812
Chasidic rebbe, halachic authority, and founder of the Chabad movement. The Alter Rebbe was born in Liozna, Belarus, and was among the principal students of the Magid of Mezeritch. His numerous works include the *Tanya*, an early classic containing the fundamentals of Chabad Chasidism, and *Shulchan Aruch HaRav*, an expanded and reworked code of Jewish law.

guarantor. [Therefore] he is considered obligated in this matter, as long as his fellow has not fulfilled his own obligation.

One Entity

TEXT 10

Rabbi Shneur Zalman of Liadi, Likutei Torah, Beha'alotecha 33c

ויש להקדים תחלה ענין מה שנקראו כנסת ישראל מנורה כי כמו שהמנורה היא "מקשה אחת תעשה המנורה", שעל ידי המקשה שמקישים אותה נעשה מה שלמעלה למטה ומה שלמטה למעלה ונתערב הכל עליון בתחתון ותחתון בעליון. כך "כל ישראל ערבים זה בזה", כלומר מעורבים זה בזה כי "אתם קרוים אדם", כמו האדם שיש לו ראש ורגל, והראש מקבל חיות גם מהרגל שצריך לו, כך כל ישראל ביחד הם נקראים אדם אחד קומה אחת.

We ought to explain why the collective of the Jewish people are referred to as a menorah candelabra:

The menorah is [as the verses states,] "To be made of one beaten [piece of gold]." Typically, when something is beaten, that which is above [is sent] below, and that which is below is above, so that everything is mixed (nit'arev) together, high and low, low and high. So it is that "all of Israel are guarantors (arevim)," that is to say they are mixed up (me'urav) with each other.

So it is said [of the Jewish people], "You are called Man." For just as a man possesses a head and feet, and the head receives life-force from the feet, for it relies on them, so, too, is the entire Jewish people together called one singular Man, one entity.

TEXT 11

The Lubavitcher Rebbe, Likutei Sichot, vol. 30, p. 217

כמו כן הוא לענין חיוב ממון, שמצד דין ערבות דכל ישראל ערבין זה בזה, חיוב תשלומין שעל הלוה חל על חבירו הערב כאילו הוא לוה המעות ונתחייב בתשלום חוב זה.

So it is regarding monetary debt. On account of the principle of arvut, that "all of Israel are guarantors for one another," the borrower's duty of repayment falls on his fellow, the guarantor, as though he had borrowed the money himself, and incurred this debt.

We're All in this Together

Judah's Pledge

TEXT 12

Rashi, Bereishit 44:32

"כי עבדך ערב את הנער". ואם תאמר למה אני נכנס לתגר יותר משאר
אחי, הם כולם מבחוץ, אבל אני נתקשרתי בקשר חזק להיות מנודה
בשני עולמות.

"For your servant assumed responsibility for the boy." Now, if you ask why I enter the fray more than my other brothers, [I will reply that] they are all [standing] from the outside [without commitment], while I have bound myself with a strong bond to be an outcast in both worlds.

Out of Many, One

TEXT 13

Rabbi Shlomo ben Aderet, Responsa of the Rashba, vol. I, §148

המלך כצבור שהצבור וכל ישראל תלויין בו.

The king is like the community, because the community, and all of Israel, are dependent on him.

TEXT 14

Rashi, Bamidbar 21:21

שמשה הוא ישראל וישראל הם משה, לומר לך שנשיא הדור הוא ככל הדור, כי הנשיא הוא הכל.

Moses is Israel, and Israel is Moses, to teach you that the leader (nasi) of the generation is equal to the entire generation, because the leader is everything.

Rabbi Shlomo Yitzchaki (Rashi)
1040–1105
Most noted biblical and Talmudic commentator. Born in Troyes, France, Rashi studied in the famed *yeshivot* of Mainz and Worms. His commentaries on the Pentateuch and the Talmud, which focus on the straightforward meaning of the text, appear in virtually every edition of the Talmud and Bible.

TEXT 15

Bereishit (Genesis) 49:9-10

גּוּר אַרְיֵה יְהוּדָה מִטֶּרֶף בְּנִי עָלִיתָ כָּרַע רָבַץ כְּאַרְיֵה וּכְלָבִיא מִי יְקִימֶנּוּ: לֹא יָסוּר שֵׁבֶט מִיהוּדָה וּמְחֹקֵק מִבֵּין רַגְלָיו עַד כִּי יָבֹא שִׁילֹה וְלוֹ יִקְּהַת עַמִּים:

A cub [and] a grown lion is Judah. From the prey, my son, you withdrew. He crouched, rested like a lion, and like a lion, who will rouse him?

The scepter shall not depart from Judah, nor the student of the law from between his feet, until Shiloh comes, and to him will be a gathering of peoples.

Never Alone

TEXT 16

Midrash Vayikra Rabah, Vayikra 4:6

תני רבי שמעון בר יוחאי: משל לבני אדם, שהיו יושבין בספינה נטל
אחד מהן מקדח והתחיל קודח תחתיו. אמרו לו חבריו: מה אתה יושב
ועושה?! אמר להם: מה אכפת לכם לא תחתי אני קודח?! אמרו לו:
שהמים עולין ומציפין עלינו את הספינה

Rabbi Shimon bar Yochai taught: There is a parable of two people who were sitting on a ship. One of them took a drill, and began to drill beneath him.

His friends said to him, "What are you sitting and doing?"

He said to them, "Why are you concerned? Am I not drilling beneath my own place?"

They said to him, "Because the waters will rise up and flood the boat for all of us!"

Vayikra Rabah
An early rabbinic commentary on the Book of Leviticus. This Midrash, written in Aramaic and Hebrew, provides textual exegeses and anecdotes, expounds upon the biblical narrative, and develops and illustrates moral principles. It was first printed in Constantinople in 1512 together with four other Midrashic works on the other four books of the Pentateuch.

When Is Moshiach Coming?

Growing Out of the Exile Mentality

Dedicated by the JLI team in honor of the birthday of Reb Shmuel Goodman, 14 Teves
May he and his family merit the fulfillment of continuous blessings for health, happiness, nachas and success in all endeavors.

PARASHA OVERVIEW
Vayechi

Jacob lives the final 17 years of his life in Egypt. Before his passing, he asks Joseph to take an oath that he will bury him in the Holy Land. He blesses Joseph's two sons, Manasseh and Ephraim, elevating them to the status of his own sons as progenitors of tribes within the nation of Israel.

The patriarch desires to reveal the end of days to his children, but is prevented from doing so.

Jacob blesses his sons, assigning to each his role as a tribe: Judah will produce leaders, legislators and kings; priests will come from Levi, scholars from Issachar, seafarers from Zebulun, schoolteachers from Simeon, soldiers from Gad, judges from Dan, olive-growers from Asher, and so on. Reuben is rebuked for "confusing his father's marriage bed"; Simeon and Levi, for the massacre of Shechem and the plot against Joseph. Naphtali is granted the swiftness of a deer, Benjamin the ferociousness of a wolf, and Joseph is blessed with beauty and fertility.

A large funeral procession consisting of Jacob's descendants, Pharaoh's ministers, the leading citizens of

Egypt and the Egyptian cavalry accompanies Jacob on his final journey to the Holy Land, where he is buried in the Machpelah Cave in Hebron.

Joseph, too, dies in Egypt, at the age of 110. He, too, instructs that his bones be taken out of Egypt and buried in the Holy Land, but this would come to pass only with the Israelites' exodus from Egypt many years later. Before his passing, Joseph conveys to the Children of Israel the testament from which they will draw their hope and faith in the difficult years to come: "G-d will surely remember you, and bring you up out of this land to the land of which He swore to Abraham, Isaac and Jacob."

The Big Secret

Introduction

TEXT 1

Letter of The Ba'al Shem Tov, printed in "Ben Porat Yosef,"
by Rabbi Ya'akov Yosef of Polnoye

בראש השנה שנת תק"ז עשיתי השבעת עליית הנשמה, כידוע לך,
וראיתי דברים נפלאים במראה מה שלא ראיתי עד הנה מיום עמדי על
דעתי... ועליתי מדרגה אחר מדרגה עד שנכנסתי להיכל משיח ששם
לומד משיח תורה עם כל התנאים והצדיקים... ושם ראיתי שמחה גדולה
עד מאד... והייתי סובר שהשמחה הזו חס ושלום על פטירתי מהעולם
הזה והודיעו לי אחר כך שאיני נפטר עדיין כי הנאה להם למעלה כשאני
מייחד יחודים למטה...

ושאלתי את פי משיח: אימת אתי מר? והשיב: בזאת תדע, בעת
שיתפרסם למודך ויתגלה בעולם ויפוצו מעיינותיך חוצה... ותמהתי על
זה והיה לי צער גדול באריכות הזמן כל כך, מתי זה אפשר להיות?

Rabbi Yaakov Yosef of Polnoye
ca. 1710–1784

Chasidic pioneer and author. Rabbi Yaakov Yosef was a dedicated disciple of the Baal Shem Tov, the founder of the Chasidic movement, and is credited with taking a leading role in the dissemination of the philosophy of Chasidism in its nascent years. He authored *Toledot Yaakov Yosef*, the first printed work of Chasidic philosophy. This work is cherished in Chasidic circles.

On Rosh Hashanah of the year 5507, I performed, by means of oath, an elevation of soul [to the higher spiritual realms], as known to you, and saw wondrous things I had never seen before... I ascended from level to level until I entered the chamber of the Moshiach where he learns Torah with all the Sages and the righteous...

I saw great joy there... At first I thought that the reason for this joy was because I had passed away from the physical world, Heaven forbid. Later, they told me *that my time had not yet come to die, since they have great pleasure on High from what I am doing below...*

I asked the Moshiach, "When will the Master come?" He answered, "This is how you will know: When your teaching will become public and revealed in the world, and your wellsprings will burst forth to the farthest extremes..."

I was stunned and distressed; this could be so long— when will it just finally be?!

Jacob's Wish

TEXT 2A

Bereishit (Genesis) 49:1

וַיִּקְרָא יַעֲקֹב אֶל בָּנָיו וַיֹּאמֶר הֵאָסְפוּ וְאַגִּידָה לָכֶם אֵת אֲשֶׁר יִקְרָא אֶתְכֶם בְּאַחֲרִית הַיָּמִים:

Jacob called for his sons and said, "Gather and I will tell you what will happen to you at the end of days."

TEXT 2B

Rabbi Shlomo Yitzchaki
(Rashi)
1040–1105
Most noted biblical and
Talmudic commentator.
Born in Troyes, France,
Rashi studied in the famed
yeshivot of Mainz and
Worms. His commentaries
on the Pentateuch and
the Talmud, which focus
on the straightforward
meaning of the text, appear
in virtually every edition
of the Talmud and Bible.

Rashi ad loc.

"ואגידה לכם." בקש לגלות את הקץ ונסתלקה ממנו שכינה והתחיל אומר דברים אחרים.

And I will tell you." He attempted to reveal the (end of the Exile), but the Shechinah withdrew from him. So he began to say other things.

Secrets of Life

TEXT 3

Talmud Tractate Pesachim, 54B

תנו רבנן שבעה דברים מכוסים מבני אדם אלו הן יום המיתה ויום
הנחמה ועומק הדין ואין אדם יודע מה בלבו של חבירו ואין אדם יודע
במה משתכר ומלכות בית דוד מתי תחזור ומלכות חייבת מתי תכלה.

ur Rabbis taught: Seven things are hidden from mankind:

1. The day of death

2. The day of consolation

3. The exactness of judgment

4. What another person is thinking

5. How a person will earn a living

6. When the Kingdom of David will return

7. When the evil rule will end

Babylonian Talmud
A literary work of monumental proportions that draws upon the legal, spiritual, intellectual, ethical, and historical traditions of Judaism. The 37 tractates of the Babylonian Talmud contain the teachings of the Jewish sages from the period after the destruction of the 2nd Temple through the 5th century CE. It has served as the primary vehicle for the transmission of the Oral Law and the education of Jews over the centuries; it is the entry point for all subsequent legal, ethical, and theological Jewish scholarship.

The Purpose of the Blessings

The Future Tribes

TEXT 4A

Rabbi Eliyahu Mizrachi, Re'em to Rashi, Bereishit 49:1

לא ידעתי מי הכריחם לומר זה? ולמה לא יהיה "ואגידה לכם את אשר יקרא אתכם"—על הדברים העתידים לבוא לכל שבט ושבט?

I don't understand what compelled Rashi to say this. Why can't the words "I will tell you what will happen to you" be understood as a reference to what will happen in the future to each of the tribes?

TEXT 4B

Rabbi Shmuel ben Meir
(Rashbam)
1085–1158

Talmudist and biblical commentator. Rashbam was born in Troyes, France, to Yocheved, the daughter of Rashi. Rashbam, a prominent member of the Tosafists, authored commentaries on the Pentateuch and the Talmud. Like his grandfather's, Rashbam's commentaries focus on the plain meaning of the Talmudic and biblical texts.

Rabbi Shmuel ben Meir, Pirush Harashbam, Bereishit 49:1

"באחרית הימים". עניין גבורתם ונחלתם.

"At the end of days." Their strength and inheritances.

Two Gatherings

TEXT 5A

Bereishit (Genesis) 49:1

וַיִּקְרָא יַעֲקֹב אֶל בָּנָיו וַיֹּאמֶר הֵאָסְפוּ וְאַגִּידָה לָכֶם אֵת אֲשֶׁר יִקְרָא אֶתְכֶם
בְּאַחֲרִית הַיָּמִים:

acob called for his sons and said, "Gather and I will tell you what will happen to you at the end of days."

TEXT 5B

Ibid. 49:2

הִקָּבְצוּ וְשִׁמְעוּ בְּנֵי יַעֲקֹב וְשִׁמְעוּ אֶל יִשְׂרָאֵל אֲבִיכֶם:

ather and listen, sons of Jacob, and listen to Israel, your father.

TEXT 5C

Rabbi Shlomo Ephraim Luntschitz, Keli Yakar ad loc.

לשון אסיפה שייך למי שעומד בחוץ במקום מגולה ונאסף לתוך הבית למקום צנוע, כמו, "ואספתו אל תוך ביתך", "ואין איש מאסף אותי הביתה", וכן רבים. אבל לשון קיבוץ מורה על אנשים מפוזרים שיתקבצו למקום אחד אפילו שיהיה במקום מגולה ובקעי בו רבים. כך מתחילה ביקש לגלות סוד הקץ ואין ראוי לגלות דבר סוד ברשות הרבים פן ישמע מי שאינו הגון, כי סוד ה' ליראיו דוקא, על כן אמר האספו ואגידה לכם את אשר יקרא אתכם באחרית הימים לעת קץ, ומיד הרגיש בעצמו שנסתם ממנו הקץ, על כן חזר מלשון אסיפה ואמר הקבצו בני יעקב לשמוע דברים שאין בהם סוד ויכול לדבר ממנו ברבים.

Rabbi Shlomo Ephraim of Luntschitz
1550–1619

After studying in the yeshivah of the Maharshal, Rabbi Shlomo Ephraim gained a reputation as a distinguished preacher and scholar. He traveled far and wide to deliver his fiery sermons, which were collected and published. He is primarily known today for his work *Keli Yakar*, and for his commentary on the Pentateuch, which was subsequently printed in many editions of the Bible.

The term applies to one situated in a public place who then moves inside to a more private place, as in the verse "you shall bring it into your house," and "and no one takes me home." But the term refers to people spread out who merely gather together, even if it will be out in the open.

At first, Jacob wished to reveal to his children the time of Moshiach's arrival, and such a secret cannot be revealed in a public place lest someone unworthy hear it, for "a secret of G-d is [only] for those who fear Him." Therefore, he said, "Gather [הֵאָסְפוּ] and I will tell you what will happen to you at the end of days." Immediately he felt that the matter was hidden from him so he changed his wording and said, "Gather [הִקָּבְצוּ] and listen, sons of Jacob," to hear words that are not secret and can be spoken in public.

Calculating End Times

A Beacon of Hope

TEXT 6

Maimonides, Iggeret Teiman

אנחנו נתנצל בשם רבנו סעדיה [גאון] ז"ל [שחישב קיצים] ונאמר שלמרות שהוא ידע שאסור לעשות כן, מה שהביאו לעשות זאת היא היות אנשי דורו מלאי ספקות באמונה, וכמעט שאבדה דת ה', לולי היה הוא ז"ל... לקבץ המון בני האדם בחשבון הקצים, לחזקת תוחלתם לאמת.

*I*n defense of Rabbi Saadiah Gaon, of blessed memory, who calculated end times: Though he knew this practice is frowned upon, he was compelled to do so for the people of his generation were full of crises of faith and would have all but given up the Jewish religion if not for him... uniting the masses by calculating end times, to truly strengthen their hope.

Rabbi Moshe ben Maimon
(Maimonides, Rambam)
1135–1204

Halachist, philosopher, author, and physician. Maimonides was born in Cordoba, Spain. After the conquest of Cordoba by the Almohads, he fled Spain and eventually settled in Cairo, Egypt. There, he became the leader of the Jewish community and served as court physician to the vizier of Egypt. He is most noted for authoring the *Mishneh Torah*, an encyclopedic arrangement of Jewish law, and for his philosophical work, *Guide for the Perplexed*. His rulings on Jewish law are integral to the formation of halachic consensus.

TEXT 7

Rabbi Yehudah Loew
(Maharal of Prague)
1525–1609

Talmudist and philosopher.
Maharal rose to prominence
as leader of the famed Jewish
community of Prague. He
is the author of more than
a dozen works of original
philosophic thought, including
Tiferet Yisrael and *Netzach
Yisrael.* He also authored *Gur
Aryeh,* a supercommentary to
Rashi's biblical commentary,
and a commentary on the non-
legal passages of the Talmud.
He is buried in the Old
Jewish Cemetery of Prague.

Rabbi Yehuda Loew, Netzach Yisrael, end of ch. 40

תדע שכל מה שאמרו חכמים בעניין הקץ, לא שהיו גוזרים שכך
היה בודאי באותו זמן ובאותה שעה, רק שגילה לנו זמן מוכן שראוי
שיהיה בו הקץ... הקץ הוא מהדברים הנעלמים אשר אי אפשר שיהיה
נגלה בברור.

When the Sages predicted a keitz it's not as if they were definitively **decreeing** that it will come at that given time and hour. Rather, they revealed to us a time that was ripe for the keitz to occur... The Keitz is one of those secret matters that cannot be revealed definitively.

History of Given End-Times

TEXT 8A

Daniel 12:5-13

רָאִיתִי אֲנִי דָנִיֵּאל וְהִנֵּה שְׁנַיִם אֲחֵרִים עֹמְדִים אֶחָד הֵנָּה לִשְׂפַת הַיְאֹר
וְאֶחָד הֵנָּה לִשְׂפַת הַיְאֹר:
וַיֹּאמֶר לָאִישׁ לְבוּשׁ הַבַּדִּים אֲשֶׁר מִמַּעַל לְמֵימֵי הַיְאֹר עַד מָתַי קֵץ הַפְּלָאוֹת:
וָאֶשְׁמַע אֶת הָאִישׁ לְבוּשׁ הַבַּדִּים אֲשֶׁר מִמַּעַל לְמֵימֵי הַיְאֹר וַיָּרֶם יְמִינוֹ
וּשְׂמֹאלוֹ אֶל הַשָּׁמַיִם וַיִּשָּׁבַע בְּחֵי הָעוֹלָם כִּי לְמוֹעֵד מוֹעֲדִים וָחֵצִי וּכְכַלּוֹת
נַפֵּץ יַד עַם קֹדֶשׁ תִּכְלֶינָה כָל אֵלֶּה:
וַאֲנִי שָׁמַעְתִּי וְלֹא אָבִין וָאֹמְרָה אֲדֹנִי מָה אַחֲרִית אֵלֶּה:
וַיֹּאמֶר לֵךְ דָנִיֵּאל כִּי סְתֻמִים וַחֲתֻמִים הַדְּבָרִים עַד עֵת קֵץ:

יִתְבָּרְרוּ וְיִתְלַבְּנוּ וְיִצָּרְפוּ רַבִּים וְהִרְשִׁיעוּ רְשָׁעִים וְלֹא יָבִינוּ כָּל רְשָׁעִים וְהַמַּשְׂכִּלִים יָבִינוּ:

וּמֵעֵת הוּסַר הַתָּמִיד וְלָתֵת שִׁקּוּץ שֹׁמֵם יָמִים אֶלֶף מָאתַיִם וְתִשְׁעִים:

אַשְׁרֵי הַמְחַכֶּה וְיַגִּיעַ לְיָמִים אֶלֶף שְׁלֹשׁ מֵאוֹת שְׁלֹשִׁים וַחֲמִשָּׁה:

וְאַתָּה לֵךְ לַקֵּץ וְתָנוּחַ וְתַעֲמֹד לְגֹרָלְךָ לְקֵץ הַיָּמִין:

And I, Daniel, saw, and behold two others were standing, one on this side of the river bank, and one on that side of the riverbank.

And he said to the man clad in linen, who was above the waters of the river, "How long will it be until the secret end?"

And I heard the man clad in linen, who was above the waters of the river, and he raised his right hand and his left hand to the heavens, and he swore by the Life of the world, that in the time of [two] times and a half, and when they have ended shattering the strength of the holy people, all these will end.

And I heard, but I did not understand, and I said, "My lord, what is the end of these?"

And from the time the daily sacrifice was removed and the silent abomination placed, is 1,290.

Fortunate is he who waits and reaches days of 1,335.

And you, go to the end, and you will rest and rise to your lot at the end of the days.

TEXT 8B

Rashi ad loc.

אלף מאתים ותשעים שנה הן מיום הוסר התמיד [ימי החורבן השני] עד שישוב בימי משיחנו.

1,290 years from the time the tamid *offering ceased [at the destruction of the Second Temple] until it will return with the coming of* Moshiach.

TEXT 8C

Rabbi Moshe ben Nachman
(Nachmanides, Ramban)
1194–1270
Scholar, philosopher, author and physician. Nachmanides was born in Spain and served as leader of Iberian Jewry. In 1263, he was summoned by King James of Aragon to a public disputation with Pablo Cristiani, a Jewish apostate. Though Nachmanides was the clear victor of the debate, he had to flee Spain because of the resulting persecution. He moved to Israel and helped reestablish communal life in Jerusalem. He authored a classic commentary on the Pentateuch and a commentary on the Talmud.

Nachmanides, Pirush Haramban, Bereishit 5:8

ויהיה זה קיח שנה אחר האלף החמישי ... מעת הוסר התמיד לתת שיקוץ שומם ימים אלף מאתים ותשעים.

This will be in the Hebrew year 5118… for from the time the tamid *offering ceased until its restoration are 1290 years.*

TEXT 9

Maimonides, Iggeret Teiman

יש אצלנו קבלה גדולה ונפלאת... שתתחזור הנבואה לישראל ... בשנת ד׳ תתקע"ו ליצירה (1216=), ואין ספק שחזרת הנבואה היא הקדמת המשיח ... זהו יותר אמיתי מכל חשבון שנאמר בשום קץ.

We have a wonderful and expansive tradition… that prophecy will return to Israel… in the Hebrew year 4976 [1216 on the secular calendar]. It is without doubt that the return of prophecy is a precursor to Moshiach… this is more accurate than any other calculated end-time.

"Merit" or "No Merit"

TEXT 10A

Talmud Tractate Sanhedrin 98a

רבי יהושע בן לוי רמי כתיב "בעתה" וכתיב "אחישנה"? —זכו, אחישנה; לא זכו, בעתה.

אמר רבי אלכסנדרי רבי יהושע בן לוי: רמי, כתיב "וארו עם ענני שמיא כבר אינש אתה" וכתיב "עני ורוכב על חמור"? זכו עם ענני שמיא לא זכו עני רוכב על חמור.

Rabbi Yehoshua ben Levi asked: It is written [regarding Moshiach's arrival], "In its time," yet the verse continues, "I will hasten it"!

[The answer is:] If the Jewish people are worthy, "I will hasten it." But if they are not, the redemption will come "in its time."

Rabbi Aleksandri said in the name of Rabbi Yehoshua ben Levi: It is written, "And behold, with the clouds of the heaven, one like a man was coming," but elsewhere it is written, "humble and riding a donkey."

[The answer is:] If the Jewish people are worthy, Moshiach will come "with the clouds of the heaven." But if they are not, he will come as one "humble and riding a donkey."

TEXT 10B

Talmud, ibid.

רבי יהושע בן לוי אשכח לאליהו דהוי קיימי אפיתחא דמערתא דרבי שמעון בן יוחאי אמר ליה ... אימת אתי משיח? אמר ליה זיל שייליה לדידיה. והיכא יתיב? אפיתחא דקרתא. ומאי סימניה? יתיב ביני עניי סובלי חלאים וכולן שרו ואסירי בחד זימנא איהו שרי חד ואסיר חד. אמר דילמא מבעינא דלא איעכב. אזל לגביה אמר ליה שלום עליך רבי ומורי, אמר ליה שלום עליך בר ליואי. א"ל לאימת אתי מר? א"ל היום. אתא לגבי אליהו ... אמר ליה: שקורי קא שקר בי, דאמר לי היום אתינא ולא אתא. אמר לו: הכי אמר לך: היום אם בקולו תשמעו.

Rabbi Yehoshua ben Levi found Elijah the Prophet standing at the entrance to the cave of Rabbi Shimon bar Yochai. He said to him… "When will Moshiach come?" Elijah answered, "Go and ask him."

"But where is he?"

"At the entrance of the city."

"And how shall I know it is him?

"He is sitting among the poor lepers. All the others untie all their bandages at once to clean their wounds before retying them, but Moshiach *unties, cleanses, and reties one wound at a time. Thus, should he be called upon, he will not be delayed."*

Rabbi Yehoshua went to Moshiach *and said to him, "Peace upon you, my master and teacher!"* Moshiach *responded, "Peace upon you, son of Levi."*

"When will the master come?"

"Today."

*Rabbi Yehoshua went back to Elijah… He said, "*Moshiach *lied to me, for he said he would come today, but he did not come!"*

"This is what he said to you, 'Today, if you listen to G-d's voice.'"

STORY

When he would travel, the Chafetz Chaim would take a closed suitcase with him. He never opened this suitcase, yet he never left home without it. His family was always extremely curious to know what it contained, but they never succeeded in finding out.

After his passing, they opened the suitcase. Inside, they found a brand-new Yom Tov *kapoteh*. They remembered then what the Chafetz Chaim had once said, "It is appropriate to greet *Moshiach* with a new Yom Tov *kapoteh*."

Learning from the Exile Calculation

TEXT 11

The Lubavitcher Rebbe, Likutei Sichot vol. 20, p .231

ולכן יש לומר אז כוונת יעקב איז געווען: ווען אידן וועלן באם גילוי הקץ
וויסן אז עס איז תלוי אין "זכו" (כנ"ל), וועלן זיי מוסיף זיין אין זייער
"זכו" (עבודת ה'), וועט די הוספה **מקדים** זיין די גאולה, אז זי זאל קומען
נאך פאר דעם באשטימטן קץ, על דרך מאמר חז"ל: "זכו—אחישנה".
ועל דרך ווי מען געפינט ביי יציאת מצרים גופא: איינער פון די טעמים
וואס גלות מצרים האט געדויערט נאר רד"ו שנה—ניט ארבע מאות
שנה ווי סאיז געווען באשטימט בברית בין הבתרים—איז ווייל דער
קושי השעבוד האט משלים געווען דעם מנין (פון ארבע מאות שנה);
איז מובן אז כשם ווי די הוספה אין שעבוד (**קושי** השעבוד) האט
מקדים געווען די גאולה—על דרך זה (ובמכל שכן) וואלט זיך דאס
אויפגעטאן דורך דער הוספה אין "זכו", אין טובה.

Rabbi Menachem Mendel Schneerson
1902–1994

The towering Jewish leader of the 20th century, known as "the Lubavitcher Rebbe," or simply as "the Rebbe." Born in southern Ukraine, the Rebbe escaped Nazi-occupied Europe, arriving in the U.S. in June 1941. The Rebbe inspired and guided the revival of traditional Judaism after the European devastation, impacting virtually every Jewish community the world over. The Rebbe often emphasized that the performance of just one additional good deed could usher in the era of Moshiach. The Rebbe's scholarly talks and writings have been printed in more than 200 volumes.

Jacob's intention was this: If the Jewish people would know that Moshiach's arrival is hinged upon their merit, they would increase their Divine service so as to hasten the redemption before its set time, as the Talmud states, "If the Jewish people are worthy, I will hasten it."

Indeed, so it was in the exodus from Egypt: One of the reasons the Jews were enslaved for 210 years—instead of the 400 years set at the Covenant of the Parts—is that the harshness of their slavery made up what was lacking in years.

If the harshness of slavery caused the exodus from Egypt to come sooner, certainly an increase in good deeds will bring the redemption sooner.

Wanting Moshiach

A great sage was traveling and took lodging at a small inn owned by a simple Jewish couple. Very early in the morning, he arose for *tikkun chatzot*, to mourn the destruction of the Temple and pray for the coming of *Moshiach*.

Hearing the noise, the innkeeper went to see what was happening.

The sage explained that he was praying for *Moshiach* to come and take all the Jews to the Holy Land.

Amazed at this idea, the innkeeper went to tell his wife the news that *Moshiach* would soon come to redeem the Jewish people. "But we are settled here," she said.

"We've just finished paying off the inn and just purchased a new cow for its milk. Must we now pick up and leave everything behind?"

Confused, the innkeeper went back to the sage to relay his wife's concerns. "Don't you understand?" asked the sage, "When *Moshiach* comes, all our suffering will end. No more persecution, no more pogroms, and no more anti-Semitic landlord to torment you!"

Enthused, the innkeeper rushed back to his wife with the good news. But she was adamant: "Tell the rabbi he should take all the anti-Semitic goyim to Israel with *Moshiach*, and leave us here in peace!"

Eternal Redemption

TEXT 12

The Lubavitcher Rebbe, Likutei Sichot vol. 20 p. 232

כאשר העבודה נעשית מצד סיוע מלמעלה ולא ביגיעת עצמו, הרי
אז אין "נצחיות" בעבודה, כאשר הסיוע האלוקי יתעלם, יכול האדם
לרדת ממדרגתו ח"ו. דווקא בשעה שהעבודה באה באתערותא דלתתא
(בכוח עצמו), היא בבחינת דבר המתקיים ומביאה גאולה נצחית שאין
אחריה גלות.

When one's G-dly service is done with Divine input, and not with his own efforts, it will not endure, for once the Divine assistance ceases he will naturally fall from his current level.

Only when one's service is done by his own efforts will it endure and bring about the final, everlasting redemption after which there can be no exile.

Asking for Moshiach

TEXT 13A

Talmud Tractate Shabbat 31a

אמר רבא: בשעה שמכניסין אדם לדין [בבית דין של מעלה], אומרים לו: נשאת ונתת באמונה? קבעת עתים לתורה? עסקת בפו"ר? ציפית לישועה?

Rava said: When a person comes to the Heavenly Court, he is asked: Were your business dealings honest? Did you set time for Torah study? Did you yearn for redemption?

TEXT 13B

Maimonides, Mishneh Torah, Laws of Kings, 11:2

וכל מי שאינו מאמין בו או שאינו מחכה לביאתו לא בשאר נביאים בלבד הוא כופר אלא בתורה ובמשה רבינו.

Anyone who does not believe in the Moshiach or does not await his coming denies not only the statements of the other prophets, but those of the Torah and Moses, our teacher.

Revisiting Jacob

TEXT 14

The Lubavitcher Rebbe, Likutei Sichot ibid.

יעקב רצה שנצא כמה שיותר מהר מהגלות. יתכן אמנם שיהיה חסר
בשלמות הגאולה, אבל הגאולה עצמה תבוא בהקדם. וזהו דיוק הלשון
"ביקש יעקב לגלות", מלשון "בקשה", יעקב התכוון לבקש בכך מהקב"ה
את זירוז גילוי הקץ.

אולם הקב"ה רוצה שהגאולה תבוא בתכלית השלמות – שזה קשור
בכך שעבודת היהודים להביא את משיח תהיה בשלמות, ולכן 'נסתלקה
ממנו שכינה', שזה מביא לשלימות גדולה יותר בהבאת הגאולה.

Jacob wanted us simply to leave the exile as soon as possible. Perhaps the redemption would not be the most complete, but it would come quickly. This is the meaning of "ביקש"—as in a "בקשה"—a request. Jacob's intention was to request from G-d to hasten the coming of the end time.

But G-d wants the redemption to be perfectly complete, which can only happen if the Jewish people's efforts to hasten its arrival is also complete. Therefore, "The Shechinah *departed from him*" to allow for a more complete redemption.

STORY

After the fall of Napoleon in 1813-14, there was a sense among some of the Chassidic masters of the day that the arrival of *Moshiach* was imminent. They agreed among themselves that Rabbi Yaakov Yitzchak of Peshischa, the *"Yid Hakadosh,"* would depart this world and do his part in heaven to make the redemption a reality. At the same time, Yaakov Yitzchak of Lublin, the "Chozeh," and Rabbi Yisroel Hopsztajn, the "Maggid of Kozhnitz," would remain in this world to do their part. They established that the proper day for *Moshiach* to come would be Simchat Torah, 5775, or 1814.

When the day arrived, after *hakafot*, the Chozeh went into his study and asked his wife to keep a close eye on him. But, just then, there was a knock at the door, and her attention was diverted for a moment as she went to answer it. When she returned to his room, her husband was not to be found.

Hearing her cries, the Chassidim ran to see what had happened. They were horrified to find him lying on the ground, far away from the house. From that fall he became very ill, and would say that his fall came from Above for his trying to rush the redemption before its time.

THE ROHR
Jewish Learning Institute

822 Eastern Parkway, Brooklyn, New York 11213

An affiliate of
Merkos L'Inyonei Chinuch
The Educational Arm of the Worldwide
Chabad Lubavitch Movement

JEWISH LEARNING INSTITUTE

THE JEWISH LEARNING MULTIPLEX
Brought to you by the Rohr Jewish Learning Institute

In fulfillment of the mandate of the Lubavitcher Rebbe, of blessed memory,
whose leadership guides every step of our work,
the mission of the Rohr Jewish Learning Institute is to transform
Jewish life and the greater community through the study of Torah,
connecting each Jew to our shared heritage of Jewish learning.

While our flagship program remains the cornerstone of our organization,
JLI is proud to feature additional divisions catering to specific populations,
in order to meet a wide array of educational needs.

THE ROHR JEWISH LEARNING INSTITUTE,
a subsidiary of *Merkos L'Inyonei Chinuch*,
is the adult education arm of the Chabad-Lubavitch Movement.

Torah Studies provides a rich and nuanced encounter with the weekly Torah reading.

MyShiur courses are designed to assist students in developing the skills needed to study Talmud independently.

IN PARTNERSHIP WITH CHABAD ON CAMPUS

This rigorous fellowship program invites select college students to explore the fundamentals of Judaism.

IN PARTNERSHIP WITH CTEEN: CHABAD TEEN NETWORK

Jewish teens forge their identity as they engage in Torah study, social interaction, and serious fun.

The Rosh Chodesh Society gathers Jewish women together once a month for intensive textual study.

TorahCafe.com provides an exclusive selection of top-rated Jewish educational videos.

This yearly event rejuvenates mind, body, and spirit with a powerful synthesis of Jewish learning and community.

Mission participants delve into our nation's rich past while exploring the Holy Land's relevance and meaning today.

Select affiliates are invited to partner with peers and noted professionals, as leaders of innovation and excellence.

THE SAMI ROHR
RESEARCH INSTITUTE

Machon Shmuel is an institute providing Torah research in the service of educators worldwide.